THE COMPLETE GUIDE TO
LIVING BY THE
MOON

THE COMPLETE GUIDE TO
LIVING BY THE
MOON

a holistic approach to lunar-inspired wellness

STEPHANIE GAILING

WELLFLEET
PRESS

Inspiring | Educating | Creating | Entertaining

Brimming with creative inspiration, how-to projects, and useful information to enrich your everyday life, quarto.com is a favorite destination for those pursuing their interests and passions.

First published in 2022 by Wellfleet Press, an imprint of The Quarto Group,
142 West 36th Street, 4th Floor, New York, NY 10018, USA
T (212) 779-4972 F (212) 779-6058 www.Quarto.com

Wellfleet titles are also available at discount for retail, wholesale, promotional, and bulk purchase. For details, contact the Special Sales Manager by email at specialsales@quarto.com or by mail at The Quarto Group, Attn: Special Sales Manager, 100 Cummings Center Suite 265D, Beverly, MA 01915 USA.

10 9 8 7 6 5 4 3

ISBN: 978-1-63106-845-4

Library of Congress Control Number: 2022003761

Publisher: Rage Kindelsperger | Creative Director: Laura Drew | Art Director: Marisa Kwek |
Managing Editor: Cara Donaldson | Editor: Elizabeth You | Layout Design: Howie Severson |
Illustrations by Sosha Davis: pages 2, 6, 17, 23, 26-27, 29, 33, 35, 36-37, 38-39, 41, 45, 53, 63, 71, 79, 87, 95, 99-103, 105, 106-107, 108, 110, 118-119, 126-127, 134-135, 142-143, 150-151, 158-159, 166-167, 174-175, 182-183, 190-191, 198-199, 206-207

Printed in China

This book provides general information on various widely known and widely accepted images that tend to evoke feelings of strength and confidence. However, it should not be relied upon as recommending or promoting any specific diagnosis or method of treatment for a particular condition, and it is not intended as a substitute for medical advice or for direct diagnosis and treatment of a medical condition by a qualified physician. Readers who have questions about a particular condition, possible treatments for that condition, or possible reactions from the condition or its treatment should consult a physician or other qualified healthcare professional.

CONTENTS

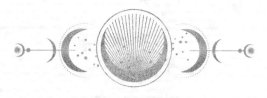

CONNECTING WITH THE MOON

Ever-present yet always changing. A beacon, guide, and timekeeper. An eternal object of our attention and affection. An inspiration as well as a destination. A companion on our nighttime journeys and an ally with whom to share our hopes, dreams, and wishes. The centerpiece of iconic works of art throughout the ages. And the home of a man, the refuge of a goddess, or the abode of a rabbit, depending upon whom you ask.

These are just some of the ways that we know the Moon.

Another is as a powerful connector. It allies us to others: as we realize that the Moon we see is the same as the one viewed throughout history, and each night by everyone around the globe, we become present to the timelessness of our shared humanity. The Moon also connects us to ourselves: as an archetypal emblem of the feminine, through it we can learn how to flow with time, align with what is nourishing, and take care of ourselves and others.

An Icon of Change and Consistency

The Moon is an agent of change. Every day, as it gains or loses light, its appearance shifts, as does the time in which we can see it overhead. As we view it moving through the sky in its varying lunar phases, we are reminded of the cycles of life, and that the nature of nature is change. The Moon has us become present to temporality and impermanence. Through it, we tap into the awareness that some periods are primed for expansion and others for reduction, and that sometimes life calls for things to be revealed while at other times concealed.

The Moon is also the epitome of consistency. Its fluctuations occur in a repetitive and reliable manner: every four weeks or so, we experience the Moon just as we had the month prior, in the same lunar phase, robed in light in the same fashion. What's more: owing to a phenomenon called synchronous rotation, we always view one of its sides and never the other, referred to as "the dark side of the Moon." That's because the time it takes to spin on its axis (27.3 days) is the same as it takes for it to orbit the Earth.

One of the many things that the Moon brings us is this: the reminder that both change and consistency are natural principles, and that they can coexist. As we acknowledge Luna's cyclicity, we can also embrace it within ourselves. As we do, we attune to a more natural rhythm, accepting that there is a reliability in life's inherent ebbs and flows.

The Moon as Timekeeper

The etymology of the word *moon* shines light on another quality with which it is afforded. It's derived from words that mean *month* and *measure*, which is not surprising given that the lunar cycle was used as an ancient timekeeping system; in fact, *month* was originally defined as the time it took from one New Moon to the next.

Since prehistoric times, people have relied upon the Moon as a timekeeper. Archaeological findings in Europe and Africa dating back to the Paleolithic period have uncovered artifacts detailing the lunar cycle. While some were etched on walls, others were on bones, which were likely ancient portable calendars—essential tools for nomadic tribes to determine when to hunt, gather, and migrate in concert with the shifting lunar luminescence.

The Gregorian calendar, the type used in most places throughout the world, is referred to as a solar calendar as it's based on the days it takes the Earth to orbit the Sun. Yet in many cultures, solilunar or lunar calendars prevail, which either partially or solely take the Moon's cycles into consideration. Examples of the former include the Chinese and Hebrew calendar. The Islamic and Māori calendars are examples of the latter.

One of the most heralded examples of the Moon's link to a period of time is to the menstrual cycle. Many find that they can keep tabs of their cycle by tracking the Moon's phases. Looking at root words can again shed light: *menstruation* is derived from a word that means *month*, which comes from a word for *moon*.

In the Moon Mapping part of the book, you'll see another way to use the Moon as a timekeeper. There you will learn about its phases and how you can use the lunar cycle for manifesting your visions and aims.

The Gravity of the Matter

Even before the principle of gravity was discovered, many philosophers and scientists correctly identified that it was the Moon that created the flow of the ocean's tides. And while the Sun does have a much larger gravitational pull, the Moon carries a stronger tidal force given its proximity to the Earth. It turns out that during New and Full Moons—when the Moon, Sun, and Earth are in alignment—the range between high and low tide is slightly larger than usual.

Just as Luna exerts a force on the ocean tides, it may also have this impact on other bodies of water. For example, it's been suggested that the movement of water in soil and plants may be impacted by the lunar cycle. This could be one of the reasons that underlies the tradition of lunar cycle–based farming practices, which are at the root of biodynamic agriculture.

Additionally, many people feel their own personal fluctuations during the month. Given that the majority of our body is composed of water, some posit that the Moon could possibly have an impact upon us as well. For example, there is a long-held belief, and a score of anecdotal evidence, that some health events are correlated with Full Moons. One of the most commonly cited associations between humans and the Moon is the way in which it may impact mental health. In fact, when the term *lunatic* came about in the thirteenth century, it did so because it was thought that both madness and epilepsy were caused by the Moon. Numerous studies have investigated whether a correlation exists between lunar phases and physical or mental health, looking at such topics as the prevalence of crime, suicide, psychiatric admissions, cardiovascular health events, and others. And while most have yet to find a correlation, others have. For example, it's suggested that Full Moon nights correspond to more traffic accidents as well as reduced sleep quality. Given the allure that the Full Moon holds, it makes sense that it will continue being a subject of inquiry in both our personal circles as well as the scientific community.

The Importance of Relationships and Perspectives

Our experience of the Moon reminds us of the fundamental importance of both relationships and perspectives, as the way we perceive it is dependent upon its orientation to other factors as well as where and when we view it. For example, while we call it moonlight, the radiance for which Luna is so well known isn't self-generated. Rather, it's a reflection of the Sun's rays shining upon the Moon. While the Sun always illuminates one side of the Moon, how much we see at any time—the phase that it is in—depends upon where the Moon is in its orbit around the Earth.

Additionally, how we perceive the Moon depends upon our point of view: where we are and when we view it. For example, as the Moon gains more light in the waxing phase, the direction by which it does so differs in the Northern and Southern Hemispheres. In the former, the light increases from the left to the right, while in the latter it does so from right to left. As such, if you were viewing a waxing Crescent Moon in Los Angeles you'd see its horns pointing left, whereas if you were witnessing it in Melbourne you'd see its horns facing right. And if you live near the equator or view it in temperate latitudes around the Equinoxes, the Crescent Moon you see usually appears like a bucket, often with the illuminated portion residing at the bottom. When it looks this way, it's often referred to as a wet Moon, smiling Moon, or even a Cheshire Moon, the latter as a nod to the grin on the cat's face in *Alice in Wonderland*.

Seeing and Being Seen

While the Sun radiates its own light and, cloud cover notwithstanding, appears in a consistent way, we cannot look upon it directly lest we risk hurting our eyes. In contrast, as variable as the Moon may be, we are always able to cast our gaze directly at it (save for when there is a Lunar Eclipse).

As we view Luna, not only do we feel connected to something mysterious and majestic, but it has us feel, even if temporarily, that we are not alone. The nursery rhyme line, *I see the Moon and the Moon sees me*, becomes our lived experience. Many people find solace when they look upon the Moon and even turn to it as a confidant of sorts, sharing their thoughts and reflections. In feeling seen, we can further recognize ourselves. This is actually one of the gifts of the astrological Moon, which we'll explore later in the book. In astrology, the location of the Moon—including the zodiac sign in which it resided when we were born—offers us great insights into our emotional needs, what makes us feel at home, and what underlies our sense of belonging. Additionally, regardless of our gender, the Moon connects us to the hallowed feminine within ourselves. Since prehistoric times, it's been associated with goddess energy, with the symbol for the archetypal triple goddess of Maiden, Mother, and Crone being composed of three lunar phases.

An iconic instance of how the Moon has helped us see ourselves better is the *Earthrise* photograph. Taken in 1968 during one of the earlier lunar orbits, it was the first color image of the Earth from space, and one that would change our collective awareness. Captured from the dark side of the Moon, it featured the Earth rising over the horizon. Through that image we could grasp the magnificence and preciousness of Gaia—and that we are all connected, all sharing the same home. *Earthrise* went on to become associated with not only a shift in global awareness but also the environmental movement.

The power of how we see the Moon is imprinted in many folkloric missives. For example, a common belief across cultures holds that the way you initially greet the New Moon augurs the events of the coming weeks. It's thought essential to view it unobstructed, and even to honor it with a greeting. Should you see it through a window, it is said to bring bad luck. And if the Moon is behind you, the way you glance at it also holds import: looking at it over your right shoulder is auspicious, while over your left is thought to bring a reversal of fortune.

The Moon Over Time

While the Moon hasn't really changed, our relationship to and understanding of it has shifted over time.

For eons, before monotheistic religions dominated, the worldview was pantheistic: nature and divinity were inseparable, and everything—whether animate or inanimate—was thought to be infused with life force. This included the Moon, which was venerated and seen as divine. Cultures throughout the world featured numerous Moon deities, such as Selene (Greek), Chang'e (Chinese), Mama Quilla (Incan), Cerridwen (Celtic), and Yemoja (Yoruba), with their myths offering a way that people could understand what this glistening sky-bound beacon symbolized. This animistic view of the Moon began to shift in antiquity when philosophers such as Anaxagoras—the first to correctly explain the origin of eclipses in the fifth century BCE—began hypothesizing a more materialistic view of the cosmos.

Given that most believed that the Earth was the center of the solar system, the Moon was often categorized as a planet, like Mercury, Venus, and the others. This understanding underwent a quantum shock in the sixteenth century when Nicolaus Copernicus, in his epic tome *On the Revolutions of the Heavenly Spheres*, proposed that the universe was heliocentric rather than geocentric. In it, he dedicated a full section to the Moon, including its orbital motion around the Earth. Owing to his work, the Moon soon came to be understood not as a planet but as a satellite.

Referring to the Moon

When you read or hear about the Moon in astrology, archetypal psychology, or other sacred arts, you often see Luna referred to using the pronouns *she/her*. That's because, as shared earlier, the Moon has been traditionally associated with goddess and feminine principles. In this book, however, I've chosen to refer to the Moon using *it/its*. The reason being: beyond the archetypal qualities the Moon embraces, as an entity it doesn't have a gender per se, and using neutral pronouns also makes it more inclusive. That said, if your relationship with the Moon is one that is infused through a different lens—if you see it as La Luna, envisioning it embodying a feminine spirit—I encourage you to continue to relate with, and refer to, the Moon as you do.

Up until the Renaissance, many people held onto the Aristotelian view that the Moon was a perfect sphere. That understanding was upended in the seventeenth century after the invention of the telescope, which the astronomer Galileo Galilei used to view the Moon, and who subsequently made detailed sketches that were published in his 1610 treatise *Starry Messenger*. After this, it became understood that rather than being uniform in shape, Luna was more egglike than perfectly circular, dotted with craters and mountains rather than having a smooth topography. An even more detailed map of the Moon would later be documented in the 1647 work *Selenography* by Johannes Hevelius.

While exploration of the Moon would be centuries away, the Earth's satellite played a pivotal role in the ease with which we could explore our own planet. As countries set out to build their maritime power to further engage in international trade, scientists looked to the Moon to help them calculate a ship's longitude, an essential tool in accurate navigation. This inspired numerous developments, including the 1675 commissioning of the Royal Observatory in England, in which astronomers could better track the position of the Moon among the fixed stars.

While the Moon was increasingly viewed through a scientific lens, it continued to capture people's imagination, including being a heralded icon in innumerable works of art. For example, it is the subject of poems by the vanguards of the Romantic movement such as Samuel Coleridge, William Wordsworth, and Percy Bysshe Shelley (the latter two both having famous poems titled *To the Moon*).

The Moon came into clearer view in the nineteenth century after the invention of daguerreotype, the earliest of the photographic processes. While its inventor, Louis Daguerre, was said to have taken the first photograph of the Moon in 1839, it was subsequently destroyed in a fire. As such, the oldest surviving lunar photograph dates to 1840, taken by physician and chemistry professor John William Draper from a rooftop in New York City. The following century we'd be introduced to even more up-close-and-personal visions of the Moon—of both the face visible to us as well as its dark side—through spacecraft-captured photographs taken in the 1950s and 1960s.

The quest to not just see the Moon but to explore it fueled our collective imagination for so long, including serving as story lines for such heralded works as Dante's *Divine Comedy* (1320), Jules Verne's *From the Earth to the Moon* (1865) and the iconic silent movie *A Trip to the Moon* (1902). However, it would take until July 20, 1969, for this dream to be realized. It was then that two American astronauts—Neil Armstrong and Edwin "Buzz" Aldrin—walked on the Moon. Ever since, there have been numerous missions to the Moon undertaken by a host of different nations.

When walking on the Moon, Armstrong captured the sentiment of this breakthrough moment in his now-famous line: "One small step for man, one giant leap for mankind." It was a paradigm-shifting historical event, setting the stage for the rapid development not only of space exploration but also technological advances. And yet, now that Luna was a place to be examined, analyzed, and perhaps even colonized, would it lead to a further loss of the Moon's age-old mystique, its allure as a divine guide and beacon of inspiration?

Thankfully, not only does the Moon continue to enchant us, recently it seems to have taken up even greater residence in our hearts and minds. We're experiencing a renaissance in subjects such as astrology, neo-paganism, Wicca, the divine feminine, and other sacred arts. And with this renaissance, talk of the Moon—whether its phases and astrological signs or the rituals, gatherings, gardening practices, and even memes dedicated to it—has become common fare.

As we quest to uncover ways to navigate our lives, both individually and collectively, we're rediscovering the Moon's inherent wisdom. Through lunar-inspired living we can capture a galaxy of understanding about how we can nurture ourselves, each other, and the planet upon which we live, the place from which we gaze upon the Moon.

Lunar-Inspired Living

The Complete Guide to Living by the Moon aims to inspire your alliance with Luna, so that you can attune to a deeper well of awareness and invoke a greater sense of holistic well-being. In it, you will find two main parts, one dedicated to Moon Mapping and the other to the Astrological Moon.

MOON MAPPING

One way to connect to the wisdom of the lunar cycles is through Moon Mapping, in which you align with the eight phases of the Moon to create aims for your life and then bring them to fruition. In this section of the book, you'll explore details of this lunar-informed stellar strategy: you'll find the invitations for growth offered by each of the lunar phases as well as self-care strategies to support you throughout the month. You'll also discover journaling guides to bolster your monthly Moon Mapping pursuits.

ASTROLOGICAL MOON

While our Sun signs offer us insights into how we shine, looking at the Moon in our astrology chart allows us access to understanding our deeper needs, what nourishes us, and how to feel a greater sense of belonging. In this section, you'll learn more about the astrological Moon through chapters dedicated to Moon signs and houses. You'll then learn about Moon Moments, which can help you to navigate periods of your life with greater awareness.

the lunar cycle and moon mapping

CHAPTER 1

AN INTRODUCTION TO MOON MAPPING

Among the many reasons that the Moon is so enchanting is that it embodies the qualities of two seemingly opposite qualities: change and consistency. Every day, as it gains or loses light, we perceive its appearance shifting. And yet, it does so consistently, in a repetitive and reliable pattern. Not only does its cyclicity make it so alluring, but it's an essential part of what gives it so much power as a beacon in our lives.

Through attuning to the lunar cycle and all of its phases, we can feel more aligned with its rhythms, which in turn can have us more connected with our own. Not only can this have us feel more in sync with each moment, but it can help us define and manifest the dreams we envision for our lives. Like our ancestors have done throughout history, through being connected to the Moon's movements, we can use it as a timekeeper as well as a guide that can help us navigate our lives. This is the heart of Moon Mapping.

The Lunar Cycle

To understand Moon Mapping, let's first look at the dynamics of the lunar cycle.

Every 29.5 days, the Moon completes a full cycle (known as a synodic month), moving from one New Moon to the next, during which it evolves from appearing devoid of the Sun's light to being fully ensconced by it, and then back again to being veiled in darkness.

NEW

BALSAMIC

CRESCENT

LAST QUARTER

FIRST QUARTER

DISSEMINATING

GIBBOUS

FULL

Note: the shape of the Moon in the diagram reflects its appearance in the Northern Hemisphere; in the Southern Hemisphere, it's a mirror image.

The two weeks in which its light increases—as it moves from New to Full Moon—is known as the waxing period. The two weeks in which its light recedes—as it moves from Full to New Moon—is called the waning period.

Each lunar cycle features eight phases. The four that are considered primary are those you see noted in calendars and almanacs: these are the New, First Quarter, Full, and Last Quarter Moons. Then there are the intermediate phases, the ones that occur between those. These are the Crescent, Gibbous, Disseminating, and Balsamic Moons.

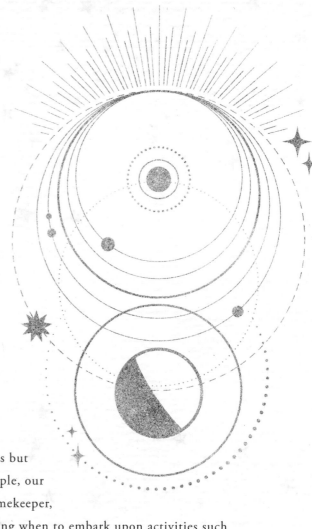

Throughout history, the Moon's phases have held sway not only over people's imaginations but also their mundane considerations. For example, our ancestors looked to the Moon as calendar, timekeeper, weather forecaster, and prompt for determining when to embark upon activities such as hunting, migrating, and holding ceremonies. Additionally, planting according to the Moon's phases has a long history. Not only is it a practice many gardeners use—and one that forms the basis of biodynamic agriculture—but there is evidence that it has been practiced as far back as ancient Egypt.

One simple way of turning to the lunar cycle for guidance is to look at whether the Moon is currently in its waxing or waning period. According to the doctrine of signatures, as the Moon's light grows during its waxing phase, we should begin projects in which expansion is heralded (e.g., launching a new business venture). Alternatively, when the Moon's light is decreasing during its waning phase, we should focus on activities in which reduction is the goal (e.g., cleaning out our closets). Yet, as you will soon see, Moon Mapping offers us much more nuanced and detailed guidance with which to navigate the month.

A Moon Mapping Guide

Each of the eight lunar phases has its own signature characteristics embodying different archetypal facets of the creative cycle. For example, when it's New Moon time, while the sky is dark, we feel the promise of potential unconstrained by limitation. Whereas when the Moon is Full, a sense of awe pervades as we perceive that a zenith has been reached with illumination showering forth. Other examples include the First and Last Quarter Moons. Situated between the New and Full Moons, they appear as turning points when we find ourselves at a crossroads and need to choose a path forward.

If we can understand the qualities inherent in each phase—and the opportunities and challenges that they bring—we can find a way to experience a greater sense of flow. One of the classic ways to frame the inherent potential of each phase is through its correspondence with a stage in the life cycle of a plant (information you can find on page 26). By recognizing the invitations each phase offers, we can choose activities that will be best supported at that moment. Moon Mapping can also inform our self-care regimens as it can help us discern which activities to pursue and when, according to the energies of the moment as well as the particular type of stress that may arise.

In addition to focusing upon the individual profiles of each of the Moon's phases, we can work with the complete lunar cycle, using it as a stellar sequencing guide for manifestation, whether in our personal or professional life. We set intentions and then thoughtfully go about bringing them to life, honoring time and the inspirations inherent within different moments. By doing so, we can take our envisioned goals, align them with the Moon, and then create a road map to actualize them. For example, Moon Mapping helps us to understand when it's the right time to create and refine an intention, embark upon concerted action, be illuminated by what we create, share acquired knowledge with others, take final steps to hone the structure of our creation, and then take a break, inviting rest and renewal.

While you'll find detailed insights into the eight lunar phases in the next chapters, the following is a synopsis of each one.

NEW MOON
✴ *Intention*

The New Moon is a time to envision what you want to create. It can be a project, a way of orienting, a new routine . . . anything you think would enhance your life. At this moment, you craft an intention, something you'd like to manifest over the next month. This is the aim that will guide you throughout the entire lunar cycle.

CRESCENT MOON
✴ *Initiation*

It's now a time to further refine and declare your intention as you begin to give shape to your New Moon vision. Through doing so, you may notice a greater sense of positivity and excitement about what you are creating. It's a time of learning and researching, as well as turning to your intuition, all of which will help you move forward in manifesting.

FIRST QUARTER MOON
✴ *Action*

Now's the moment to really dive into your endeavor. See how the committed actions you're taking and the structures you're building are setting a new course toward your future as well as away from your past. Embrace being at a turning point, working through any tension and resistance that surfaces, and learning from any confrontations you experience.

GIBBOUS MOON
✴ *Refinement*

During this phase, you begin to get powerful glimpses into how your New Moon intention is coming to life. Hopes arise as to what will manifest. With your aim in mind, apply your problem-solving skills to work through any challenges that appear. Remember that while you're close to completion, you are not there yet. It's important to stay present, have patience, and follow through.

FULL MOON

✳ *Illumination*

Clarity arrives at the Full Moon as you witness what you've created, how your New Moon intention has taken shape. You may find yourself reveling in what was generated or experiencing disappointment should the outcome not meet your expectations. Either way, consider how the way you oriented over the last two weeks contributed to what has emerged, as it offers great insights for the future.

DISSEMINATING MOON

✳ *Sharing*

This lunar phase offers you an opportunity to further understand what you have recently manifested and the process that led you there. Review and contemplation are key activities upon which to focus. It's also a potent time to gather with others, communicating and sharing your findings. Not only will they learn from you, but you will gather more knowledge by doing so.

LAST QUARTER MOON

✳ *Maturity*

It's a time to make any further adjustments necessary to the project that has been evolving over the past three weeks. Additionally, acknowledge resistance and release what you realize doesn't truly align with what you want and need. Tie up loose ends and take responsibility for what has recently occurred, including any missteps experienced along the way.

BALSAMIC MOON

✳ *Renewal*

As this current lunar cycle ends and the Moon's light fades to darkness, we move into a time of rest. It's not a period to actively start new things but to reflect upon what has been made manifest since the New Moon. Focus on activities that will replenish your mind, body, and soul. As you do, you may find yourself with whispers of what you want to give birth to in the coming lunar cycle.

A MOON MAPPING EXAMPLE

To help you further understand how to apply the principles of Moon Mapping to your own endeavors, let's consider an example. Let's say you've recently been wanting to do a crafts project, one that involves sewing a piece of clothing, and yet you haven't been certain as to exactly what you want to create. During the New Moon phase, after keeping numerous options in view, you realize that you'd really like to sew a new pair of pants. Then, during the Crescent Moon, you peruse websites featuring an array of design ideas, finally landing on one that you find attractive. When the Moon reaches its First Quarter phase, you purchase the fabrics and trimmings you need and dive into your sewing project. During the Gibbous Moon, as your design is starting to come to life, you refine your approach and attend to the details. Then, when the Full Moon lights up the sky, you get to experience the flowering of your vision and intention: your new pants! A few days later, at the Disseminating Moon, through sharing your design with others, you get accolades and feedback. You can then take these insights into the Last Quarter Moon phase, when you can make any final adjustments necessary and begin to clean up your crafts room. Finally, as the Balsamic Moon arrives, it's time to rest and take a sewing siesta, feeling grateful for what you've learned and proud of what you've created.

NEW

BALSAMIC

CRESCENT

FIRST
QUARTER

LAST
QUARTER

GIBBOUS

DISSEMINATING

FULL

Your Lunar Phase Anniversary

Each month, you may notice there is a certain period of time in which you feel a surge in energy, a sense that you have a greater level of flow. This often happens when the current lunar phase is the same one under which you were born. To determine your natal lunar phase, see page 219 in the Resources section.

HOW TO MOON MAP

In the following chapters, you will gain stellar insights into each of the eight lunar phases and how to apply the principles of Moon Mapping. There you will discover the invitations of each of the phases and how to home in on a monthly intention and then sequence the actions necessary to bring your vision to life. Plus, you'll learn about approaches that will bolster your well-being throughout the month.

In each of the lunar phase chapters, in addition to their key principles, you'll find self-care strategies, journaling prompts, action items, and a tarot card that aligns with the moment. Additionally, in the New Moon chapter, you'll discover ways to craft your monthly intention as well as how to create a ritual to support it. You will then find journaling guides that will help you work on your Moon Mapping projects.

As you Moon Map, it's important to remember the following. First, you don't need to do it every month. Just tune in around the New Moon to see if there is something you want to invite into your life, for which you will align your efforts with the lunar cycle. Sometimes you may, while other times you may not. Even if you don't want to Moon Map an endeavor in a certain month, you can always use the insights and self-care suggestions to connect to the rhythm of each of the lunar phases.

Second, remember that each monthly lunar cycle is a bigger part of an unfolding progression. As such, you will likely see connections between events and realizations that occurred in one month and how they shape what you bring to life in others. For this reason, on page 106, you will find an Intention and Manifestation Chronicle that you can use to track your developments throughout the year.

Lunar Phase Timing

When you look at a calendar or almanac, you'll notice that they denote the primary phases—the New, First Quarter, Full, and Last Quarter Moons—occurring at a specific time on a particular day. In Moon Mapping, we look to these phases, and the intermediate ones as well, not as single moments but rather as periods. We view them as beginning at a certain point and then extending for about 3.5 days, with one flowing into the next. You can find the timeline for the phases in the chart on page 26. Additionally, if you are well-versed in astrology, you can also find the time frames for each lunar phase by looking at the aspect angles between the Sun and the Moon.

QUALITIES OF THE LUNAR PHASES

Here is a reference for identifying the timeline and viewing opportunities for each of the lunar phases as well as their keywords, correspondence with a plant's life cycle, and the neo-pagan seasonal festivals associated with them.

	NEW	CRESCENT	FIRST QUARTER	GIBBOUS	FULL	DISSEMI-NATING	LAST QUARTER	BALSAMIC
ALTERNATIVE NAME		Waxing Crescent		Waxing Gibbous		Waning Gibbous	Third Quarter	Waning Crescent
TIMELINE (Days After New Moon)	0–3.7	3.7–7.4	7.4–11.1	11.1–14.8	14.8–18.5	18.5–22.1	22.1–25.8	25.8–29.5
APPEARANCE (Northern Hemisphere)								
APPEARANCE (Southern Hemisphere)								
VIEWING	Rises and sets with Sun	Rises before noon and sets before midnight	Rises around noon and sets around midnight	Rises mid-afternoon and sets after midnight	Rises around sunset and sets near sunrise	Rises after sunset and sets after sunrise	Rises around midnight and sets around noon	Rises in the pre-dawn hours and sets in the afternoon
KEYWORD	Intention	Initiation	Action	Refinement	Illumination	Sharing	Maturity	Renewal
PLANTING STAGE	Seed germinates	Seedling emerges above ground	Roots establish and stems/ leaves develop	Bud appears	Flower blooms	Flower draws bees for pollination to set fruit	Fruit is harvested, or if left on plant it begins to decay	Seeds are released from the fruit that's fallen to the ground
SEASONAL FESTIVALS	Yule, Winter Solstice	Imbolc	Ostara, Vernal Equinox	Beltane	Litha, Midsummer, Summer Solstice	Lammas, Lughnasadh	Mabon, Autumnal Equinox	Samhain

LUNAR PHASES + SUN/MOON RELATIONSHIP

Here you will find both the location of the Sun and Moon for each of the eight lunar phases as well as the associated solilunar astrological aspects that occur during each.

	NEW	CRESCENT	FIRST QUARTER	GIBBOUS	FULL	DISSEMI-NATING	LAST QUARTER	BALSAMIC
Solilunar Relationship	The Moon is 0–44° ahead of the Sun.	The Moon is 45–89° ahead of the Sun	The Moon is 90–134° ahead of the Sun	The Moon is 135–179° ahead of the Sun	The Moon is 180–134° behind the Sun	The Moon is 135–91° behind the Sun	The Moon is 90–46° behind the Sun	The Moon is 45–0° behind the Sun
Solilunar Aspects	Conjunction, Semisextile	Square, Sextile	Square, Trine	Sesqui-quadrate, Quincunx	Opposition, Quincunx	Sesqui-quadrate, Trine	Square, Sextile	Semisquare, Semisextile

CHAPTER 2

NEW MOON

INTENTION

The New Moon marks the dawn of the lunar cycle. As an origin moment, it represents all that is possible. It is the blank canvas upon which a vision will emerge. It is the inconspicuous acorn that envelops the majestic spirit of the mighty oak tree that it will become. It is the empty field, seemingly fallow and yet springing with the potential of life, as the seeds held within the soil begin to germinate.

The importance of the New Moon as a wellspring from which everything evolves is an essential notion of traditional systems of gardening. In these age-old practices, the best time to sow seeds for vegetables, fruit, and flowers that grow above ground is during this lunar phase. The reason resides not only in it being a metaphorical period in which new life is ushered in. Just as the tides are more extreme at a New Moon, it's thought that during this period more water is drawn to the Earth's surface. In turn, this creates a thriving environment in which seeds can flourish.

At this time, we connect to a sense of potentiality. We listen in for our inspirations—tuning into the waves of insight that roll over the shores of our conscious mind—to glimpse what it is that we want to make manifest. From there, we create intentions, seeds that envelop the aims of what we want to invite in over the coming month. They embody what we'd like to conceive, experience, or discover, serving as a blueprint for what we want to usher into our life.

Looking at our New Moon visions, we should ensure that it aligns with our deepest needs and reflects what we know would infuse us with a greater sense of well-being. At this lunar phase we plant the seeds of our hopes, dreams, and wishes, knowing that by mirroring the Moon's luminosity over the coming weeks, they too will grow and develop.

The Invitation: Intention

Inherent within the New Moon phase is the promise of a fresh start, the ability to expand and grow something of importance. It's the time in which we create an intention, which we can do more effectively through enhancing our vision, having space to wonder, and embracing a positive perspective.

ENHANCE YOUR VISION

As the New Moon phase begins, Luna stands directly between the Earth and the Sun, with its illuminated side hidden from view. And while the lunar face we see may be dark, that doesn't preclude us from connecting with a sense of vision, of discovering ways to see what it is we want to give birth to during this monthly lunar cycle.

Tarot Reflections: The Fool

THE FOOL

As the first card in the tarot's major arcana, the Fool embodies beginnings, just like the New Moon. It is a card of inception, which signifies unlimited potential, heralding initiating moments and reminding us that within them reside the seeds of creation. It represents the deep inspiration experienced when we connect to the burgeoning of ideas that are not limited by constraints. It embodies the experience of letting our hearts and minds wander without feeling confined to mundane considerations of whether something is practical, efficient, or doable. This card is infused with wonder, freedom, and agility. Even if the Fool doesn't yet know where they are headed, they are fully present in the moment, understanding instinctively that within it, anything is possible. They are poised to step off a proverbial cliff and to jump into a new realm, and they do so with courage and faith, knowing that the universe will support them. The Fool offers us wise guidance at the New Moon.

To first embark upon envisioning what you want to manifest, ask yourself what feels missing from your life, what shifts you'd like to make, and/or what you'd like to create. Consider what you could give birth to in the next four weeks that would feel really enriching. You can also reflect back to the past few days, during the Balsamic Moon phase (see page 90), to see if any insights that arose then relate to what you'd like to invite into your life.

After that, to gain a broader vantage point, turn to your intuition, seeing how it can direct you to what you can create this month. There are many activities that support this tune-in including: drawing, coloring, or doodling; listening to what your dreams are reflecting; taking a walk and seeing where your mind roams; working with the tarot; and/or dedicating time to journaling. Another great way to recognize what is germinating within you—to further seed your intention—is to create a vision board (see page 34). For additional approaches to discern what intention to create each month, see page 36.

SPACE TO WONDER

While the New Moon phase is when we set our intentions, it's important to remember that it's still a period in which darkness prevails. After all, while the Moon is growing in light, even by the end of this phase, it's only a whit that appears. As such, we don't necessarily want to refine every detail of our intention at this point as that may prematurely constrict its potential.

Rather, invite in spaciousness so that your intention has room to grow and naturally evolve. For example, if your relationships have not been bringing you much reward, you may find yourself with a desire to have them be more fulfilling. At this point, instead of immediately homing in on the specific friendship you'd like to see enhanced and the exact route to doing so, leave your intention more generalized, something to the extent of "I want my relationships to be more gratifying." Of course, you can still reflect upon the friendship or partnership dynamics that are currently challenging you, the ones you'd like to shift so you can find more fulfillment. Although if you allow

Solar Eclipses

Each year between two and four New Moons will be Solar Eclipses. From an astrological perspective, they are considered super-charged New Moons that usher in significant new beginnings. Often, along with the sense that something is beginning, there is a striking feeling that something is also coming to an end, so as to make space for the new that is about to take root. During Eclipses, though, clarity may seem obscured. As such, you may want to consider a different approach to Moon Mapping when doing it on a Solar Eclipse. You could find that what you're ushering in has more gravity than usual. Alternatively, you may sense that you're really not clear as to what you want to bring forth. Some people also avoid doing Solar Eclipse intention-setting because things are a bit hazy at this time. When you know that the next New Moon accords with an Eclipse, use your intuition to see how you want to approach Moon Mapping, and if you want to do it at all that month.

your intention to be broader rather than narrower during this period, you will grant yourself the time to see how it wants to naturally evolve. (You'll attend to this in the next phase, the Crescent Moon.)

POSITIVE PERSPECTIVES

As we embark upon a new lunar cycle and initiate a fresh chapter in our life, our viewpoint holds premier importance. The angle from which we perceive things has a powerful ability to inform what it is we see and the potential it has. As the New Moon is the moment when we sow the field with seeds for the future, it's especially important to pay attention to our perspective at this moment.

As such, as you craft your intentions, do so with enthusiasm and buoyant inspiration. Of course, you want to be realistic with what it is that can be brought to life in four weeks. And yet, if your usual instinct is to limit your aspirations, try to let yourself dream a little bit and stretch your vision of what you believe is possible.

Additionally, opt for positivity, rather than peppering your intention with negative beliefs. For example, you may state that you want to enhance a particular realm of your life, but if you also think you don't necessarily deserve to achieve it, you may set up a cycle of self-sabotage that can undermine even the most glorious of your intentions. When you think about how much power your outlook has, you just need to remember all the lore in which the New Moon is steeped, which emphasizes how fortune can be realized (or lost) depending upon how we view the New Moon.

STELLAR REFLECTION QUESTIONS

Here are some journaling prompts to work with during the New Moon. They can help you navigate through this time with more clarity, further connecting to the insights and awareness that this lunar phase offers.

What are my current hopes, dreams, and wishes?

....

....

How do I feel when new chapters are just beginning?

....

....

What would fill my life with greater promise and potential?

....

....

What's my vision for the next month?

....

....

What are my favorite activities for tuning into my intuition?

....

....

How can I invite in more stillness?

....

....

Self-Care Activities

We can sequence our self-care efforts during the month to align with the opportunities, challenges, and stress patterns that may inherently arise during each lunar phase. Here are several activities to practice during the New Moon.

CREATE A VISION BOARD

As shared previously, the New Moon is a time in which we begin to envision what we'd like to give birth to in the coming month. One way to tap into this aim is through creating a vision board. As the whispers of your New Moon intentions arise in your mind's eye, cut out words and images from magazines that resonate with it. Go through photographs as well as found objects—whether it be fabric, shells, charms, or other bric-a-brac—to see if any feel connected to what you are envisioning. Then arrange them in a collage and glue them to stock paper, being aware of how each connects and relates to the others. Of course, if you'd rather work digitally, you can also make a vision board filled with images you gather online. Given that the New Moon time is when you create the seed of your intention, it's important to consider your vision board a work in progress. Likely you will find yourself called to add more to it in subsequent lunar phases as you fine-tune your intention. Place your creation somewhere in your home (or on your computer) that has great visibility so that it can readily serve as a reminder of the pathway you are embarking upon this month.

YIN YOGA

While the New Moon initiates the waxing period in which we will experience growth and action, it's a lunar phase that invites quiet and inner listening. It is a time when we center ourselves so that we can discover our intentions as well as safeguard our energy in order to conserve it for the work that lies ahead. A self-care activity that can help is yin yoga, a practice in which you relax in poses for two to five minutes (or longer). Rather than focusing on increasing muscle tone, it aims to lengthen and strengthen connective tissue, including fascia, tendons, and ligaments. In turn, it bolsters the integrity of joints and bones. As you relax into the poses, you access both stillness as well as a circulation of vital life force energy. You'll feel at once centered while also enlivened, connected to the power of the present moment that the New Moon offers.

BE IN NATURE

As the Moon is steeped in darkness, and its visible light is slowly re-emerging, it calls forth a renaissance replete with the emergence of the new. Each month we have a lived experience in which we witness the juxtaposition of endings (the completion of the last lunar cycle) and beginnings (the advent of this one). A powerful way you can attune to the cycles of life that the Moon so beautifully embodies is through spending time in nature. There you can witness and experience the flora and fauna in all of its stages of development. You can become present to how even in the oldest trees or the most well-tumbled beach stones, there exists an imprint of what they were like when they first emerged. Seeing these things, you can remember that inherent in every seed—including those you are planting during the New Moon—resides the potential for great creations made manifest. Being in nature can also be really relaxing, helping you to center and clear your mind. In this quiet space, you may be able to more intuitively track emerging insights, which you can use to see what intentions want to come forth.

discerning your new moon intention

How do you discover what you would like to give birth to each month as the lunar cycle begins? Being quiet and intently listening to what's bubbling in your heart and mind is a first step. In addition to the ideas already shared in this chapter, here are several more.

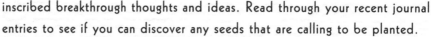

Reflect upon conversations you've had with friends where you've recounted your current wishes and desires. Survey your desk for those sticky notes upon which you inscribed breakthrough thoughts and ideas. Read through your recent journal entries to see if you can discover any seeds that are calling to be planted.

Writing is another activity that can be helpful. You could even do non-dominant handwriting, which can help you tap into the wisdom of your subconscious mind. In this practice, after asking yourself what you'd like to give birth to, begin writing your answer with the hand you usually don't use: so, if you're a righty, use your left hand to inscribe your answer, or if you're a lefty, use your right hand. This writing practice is one that can help us access insights that reside below the surface of our conscious minds, thereby expanding the field of awareness to which we can attune.

Additionally, turning to astrology may help you identify what you'd like to focus on. Each of the year's New Moons takes place in a different zodiac sign (i.e., there's an Aries New Moon, a Taurus New Moon, etc.). While each of these lunations is a time of inception, given that the sign in which the Moon resides is associated with certain themes, each of the twelve New Moons has its own signature, and therefore invites in growth in different realms of life. Below you'll find several arenas associated with each; as that particular New Moon arrives, see whether any of the motifs strikes your interest as the field in which to sow seeds for the new beginnings that you want to catalyze. You can discover a resource for finding the dates for these New Moons on page 219.

Aries New Moon
Desire
Courage
Willpower

Leo New Moon
Children
Romance
Creativity

Sagittarius New Moon
Travel
Beliefs
Adventure

Taurus New Moon
Security
Pleasure
Finances

Virgo New Moon
Health
Cleaning
Organization

Capricorn New Moon
Career
Success
Responsibility

Gemini New Moon
Education
Messaging
Communication

Libra New Moon
Beauty
Negotiations
Relationships

Aquarius New Moon
Altruism
Community
Technology

Cancer New Moon
Home
Family
Cooking

Scorpio New Moon
Sex
Emotions
Mysteries

Pisces New Moon
Spirituality
Boundaries
Compassion

Also, if you know your personal astrology chart, you can look to see where the New Moon falls within it, in which astrological house it resides, and whether it connects to any of your planets or special points. This can help you to further personalize how you want to align your New Moon intentions.

intention-setting rituals

As you envision your intention, you can simply carry it with you in your memory throughout the month. Or you may opt to write it down, or even capture it by creating a piece of art—for example, a drawing, painting, poem, or the like. Some people enjoy doing intention-setting rituals as a way to further connect to and ground their vision. If you'd like to do one, here are some ideas.

Allocate Time

Block out time on your calendar when you will do your ritual. You could do it the day when the Sun and Moon are exactly aligned (the New Moon day as marked in calendars and almanacs) or wait a day or two for when the Moon has a little bit of light. Silence your phone, shut down your computer, and let household members know that you don't want to be disturbed. Your ritual may take minutes or an hour (or more), depending upon what you want to include and what feels the most nurturing.

Clear Your Space

Put away any odds and ends used in previous activities. Use a mist made with your favorite essential oils to release negative energies in your environment. Light a candle and take out any crystals or objects you like to use for ceremony work.

Relax

Find a seat or a position that is comfortable, which will support any writing or creative activity that you may do. Take several deep breaths. Center yourself by meditating, even if only for a few minutes. If your body is feeling tight, do some yoga poses or stretching exercises. If you'd like, say a prayer or a mantra.

Open to Your Intention

Tune in to your intention and let it stream through your mind. Imagine it washing over your whole body, being infused within you. Visualize how you will feel after it has manifested. Place your intention—documented in writing or art—somewhere readily accessible so that you can stay further connected to it over the coming weeks.

Make an Altar

If you like working with altars, create one dedicated to your New Moon intention. Place objects—whether crystals, rocks, photos, or other bric-a-brac—on your altar that represent your vision, being intentional about where you put them and how they are related with one another. Never created an altar? It's simple. Just find a surface that works best for you, whether on a shelf, table, top of a bookcase, or even your nightstand. There you can place and arrange the items that will represent your intention.

Complete the Ritual

Make sure to mark the ending of your ritual. Put away any items you've been using. Thank yourself for taking the time to create space to align with your intention. Visualizing it once again, blow out the candle.

action items

- Plant seeds.
- Be positive.
- Invite in wonder.
- Let yourself wander.
- Be excited for a fresh start.
- Don't impose excess limits.
- Embrace the sense of possibility.
- Spend time in nature.
- Trust your intuition.
- Envision the new.

CHAPTER 3

CRESCENT MOON

INITIATION

The Crescent Moon is iconic. Its silhouette serves as the quintessential emblem of not only this lunar phase but as a symbolic proxy for the Moon itself. It is a popular image found in both art and artifacts, with its presence going far back to antiquity. In fact, on the Nebra Sky disc, a Bronze Age relic thought to be the earliest depiction of the cosmos, we find a Crescent Moon. And when we look to Egyptian hieroglyphics, we see it as the logogram used for the Moon. It's also emblazoned on the headdress worn by various Greco-Roman Moon Goddesses, including Diana, Artemis, and Selene. Numerous religious figures are also depicted surrounded by it: this includes the Virgin Mary, who stands upon it, and the Hindu God Shiva, who dons a Crescent Moon on his head. Furthermore, it's the astrological symbol used to represent the Moon, and its image is depicted in the High Priestess tarot card.

That the Crescent Moon is so heralded is likely due to its very recognizable appearance, more identifiable as a unique lunar image than either the circle of the New and Full Moons or semicircle of the First and Last Quarter Moons. And while these lunar phases are spoken of more often, with its widespread imagery, the image of the Crescent Moon is often the standard-bearer when it comes to depicting Luna.

Looking at its shape and burgeoning radiance allows us to understand its significance. After the darkness of the New Moon, we observe a sliver of silver light upon Luna, which will continue to grow during the waxing phase. The word itself reflects this sense of expansion; it is derived from the Latin root *crescere*, which means to gain or increase in number or strength. As we have just emerged from a period with no significant lunar evening light, as illumination returns, we can connect to the sense of hope and positivity that the Crescent Moon traditionally embodies and use this time to grow and add luster to our intentions.

The Invitation: Initiation

During the Crescent Moon, as we begin to give shape to our New Moon vision, we gain more understanding of what it is we want to achieve. As we embrace initiation, we move forward, define and distill our intention, and discover silver linings.

MOVE FORWARD

The Crescent Moon accords with the stage of the plant cycle when enough initial energy has been generated that the seedling is now able to burst forth above ground. We see the potential of life emerging from what was before only possibility. In Moon Mapping, this

Tarot Reflections: The Chariot

The Chariot card encourages us to take actions aligned with intentionality as we set out to bring our visions to life. This beautifully mirrors the invitation of the Crescent Moon. When we pull the Chariot card, we're reminded that the current moment is not a passive time but rather one in which we can access the courage and ambition we need to move forward. It reminds us that as we embark on a pathway to a new destination, if we can look within, we can access the awareness necessary to support ourselves on this journey. The Chariot signifies that it's from the depth of our intuition that we can clarify our motivations as well as learn how to fuel ourselves and chart our course. It's a card of determination and fortitude, qualities similar to that of the bull, a symbol associated with the Crescent Moon.

lunar phase is the time in which we start to slowly move our New Moon intentions forward. In this period, we take the first steps to bring form to what we've envisioned.

We derive momentum from the excitement we experience in actively participating in a creative project. Being able to see, even if ever so slightly, hints of the horizon toward which our path is heading gives us a boost while catalyzing a sense of positivity. We know in what direction we are going even if we're not presently clear what the exact route looks like. And we're fine with this, as what seems to matter is the moment and what is arising. This in and of itself gives us encouragement and infuses us with glimmers of hope.

As our intention begins to evolve, we may naturally meet obstacles. As we overcome them, we develop an increased sense of competence and capability. If you find yourself frustrated and need to marshal some strength—whether related to your New Moon intention or just in general—look no further than the symbol of the bull, a figure long associated with the crescent

shape of the Moon (given its horned form). Esteemed for their generative power, bulls have been worshipped throughout time, including serving as symbols for the Moon in ancient civilizations. During this lunar phase, channel the determination and perseverance for which the bull is known when you need to move past any stumbling blocks that are hindering your focus or confidence.

DEFINE AND DISTILL

The Crescent Moon offers us the opportunity to define and distill our visions and aims. Through seeing just how we want to breathe life into our intention, and the experiential learning that this may entail, things may come more clearly into focus. It's a time to do research, ask questions, and brainstorm. Keep an open mind and cast a wide net when it comes to the ways that you want to give form to your New Moon visions. Inventory your assets, seeing what resources and relationships may help you in your pursuits. These may be ones that not only directly help you grow your ideas but also steady you if you find yourself struggling with insecurities or doubts at this moment.

At the New Moon, we chose a target, an arena of life in which we desired to experience growth. What comes forth during this lunar phase is a clearer idea of the vehicle and pathway that will take us there. For example, if we want to enhance our sense of financial fitness, we may embark upon creating a budgeting system. Or, if we want to feel more fulfilled professionally, at the Crescent Moon we may begin to explore a new career goal. Creating a plan, crafting to-do lists, and using your calendar efficiently are some useful activities to undertake during this lunar phase. They will help sharpen your ideas as well as allow you to begin to experience the actualization of your intention.

DISCOVER SILVER LININGS

Revisiting the bull imagery, the Crescent Moon phase is one infused with bullishness, a sense of optimism and buoyancy that we can tap into for sourcing our forward movement. And during this lunar phase, marked by the Moon reflecting a trace of growing silver light, we may find ourselves more apt to see silver linings. As the Moon emerges from being steeped in darkness to visibly taking on the Sun's rays, we can more readily see the bright side of things.

As we're in the primary stages of the waxing period and things are just beginning to develop, we may have a greater ability to be flexible and adaptive. This can serve us quite well in terms of altering how we orient to situations. If we shift our position, we may be able to see things, even those that appear challenging on the surface, from a different angle, allowing us to find solutions previously unseen.

When you look at a situation, try a glass-half-full perspective on for size, seeing how it can inform you. Doing so can be helpful, notably because in the Crescent Moon phase there may be times when we encounter doubts that could stifle our forward movement. Tap into a well of positivity while still being realistic about what's in front of you.

At this juncture, another thing that is working in our favor is time. We are still at the relative beginning of the lunar cycle, with more weeks ahead to continue to bring our goals to light. Time is an asset and one of the things associated with this period. Not surprisingly, the deity Shiva, who has a strong connection to the Crescent Moon, happens to be the Hindu god of time. Remembering that time is on your side may release some pressure you're feeling and further help you to become more present to the silver linings around you.

STELLAR REFLECTION QUESTIONS

Here are some journaling prompts to work with during the Crescent Moon. They can help you navigate this time with more clarity, further connecting to the insights and awareness that this lunar phase offers.

How have I refined my New Moon intention?

....

....

What steps am I taking in its pursuit?

....

....

What stumbling blocks am I currently facing and how am I moving through them?

....

....

What resources can I turn to when I'm struggling with doubt?

....

....

How has shifting my position given me a different vantage point?

....

....

What's something that appears to be more filled with potential than I originally perceived?

....

....

Self-Care Activities

We can sequence our self-care efforts during the month to align with the opportunities, challenges, and stress patterns that may inherently arise during each lunar phase. Here are several activities to practice during the Crescent Moon.

TAKING STEPS

The Crescent Moon is a lunar phase in which you begin to take steps to move your New Moon intention forward. To inspire the momentum that this period embodies, engage in fitness activities that involve taking steps, of which there are many. Head outside for a walk, an activity that will not only get you moving but will help clear your mind. Climbing stairs not only improves lower body and core strength, but it's also a powerful cardiovascular activity. Step aerobics can be a fun exercise that provides numerous health benefits; you can find a class at your local fitness studio or purchase a low-cost platform and do it at home with an online instructional video. For an exercise that may remind you of being a kid while giving your heart a great workout, jump rope. Or step to the beat and take a dance class, or even just put on your favorite playlist and have a private dance party.

WARRIOR II YOGA POSE

During this lunar phase, we begin to have more foresight, with a budding recognition that we are embarking upon a journey to a horizon that will soon come into view. One way you can embrace a sense of this expansion is the yoga pose known as Warrior II (or *Virabhadrasana* II). In this pose, you gaze off into the distance over your outstretched arm, mindfully visualizing a goal that lies ahead. Here's how to practice it: Stand tall with your head aligned over the center of your pelvis, your arms outstretched and parallel to the floor, and your palms facing down. Walk your feet about four feet apart, rotating your right foot out ninety degrees and your left one in about thirty degrees. Bend your right knee so it is above your right foot and point your kneecap toward your middle toe. Extend your arms wide, stretching your shoulder blades while at the same time gazing over the top of your right fingertips. Stay in the pose for up to one minute, and then repeat on the other side.

CANDLE-GAZING MEDITATION

As shared earlier, one of the hallmarks of this
lunar phase is the appearance of emergent light.
With this, we move from darkness into a growing
awareness of what we are setting our sights upon
this month. A great exercise that employs the
power of light is the yogic practice of candle-
gazing meditation, also known as *trataka*. Similar
to other contemplative practices, it helps to steady
the mind and inspires relaxation. Additionally,
preliminary research suggests that it can enhance
cognitive function, reduce anxiety, and relieve insomnia.
To do this meditation practice, sit comfortably in a dark
room with a candle placed a few feet in front of you, with the flame at eye level. After closing
your eyes for a few moments, open them, setting your gaze in the middle of the flame. Try
to maintain your focus without blinking for as long as you can. Be mindful of any thoughts
that arise and try to release them. If your eyes water excessively or feel strained, close them,
envisioning the flame in your mind. Do this practice for five to ten minutes.

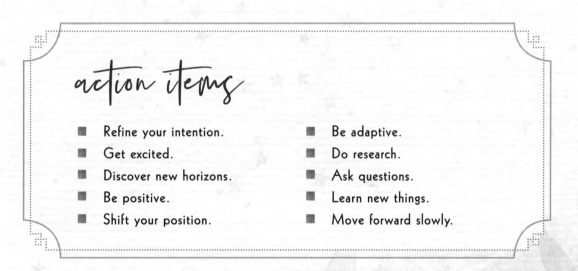

action items

- Refine your intention.
- Get excited.
- Discover new horizons.
- Be positive.
- Shift your position.
- Be adaptive.
- Do research.
- Ask questions.
- Learn new things.
- Move forward slowly.

CHAPTER 4

FIRST QUARTER MOON

ACTION

The First Quarter Moon marks an important turning point in the lunar phase. When it arrives, it signifies the moment when we are halfway through the waxing cycle, at the center of the New Moon and Full Moon.

At this betwixt-and-between point, which begins as half the Moon is bathed in light and the other in shadow, we find ourselves standing at a crossroads. Equidistant from when we planted our seed intention and when it will flower, we face important choices, the first being: Do we retreat to the past and our ingrained perspectives, even releasing our New Moon aim, or do we push forward into a new way of being and all the potential for growth it offers? This is the centerpiece of the tension that this lunar phase carries.

It's not hard to then see how the First Quarter Moon—as well as the Last Quarter Moon (see page 82)—is thought to be a time of crisis. The origin of this word can give us more insights into this period. It comes from the Greek word *krisis*, which signifies a turning point in a disease. It's the moment when two paths exist—one that leads to recovery, and one that does not. This is often how the First Quarter Moon initially feels: we sense we are at a very significant juncture and question how we will be able to channel our efforts to achieve success.

And while we may find ourselves enticed to think our way out of the quandaries we face, what's called for is taking action, the hallmark of the First Quarter Moon. Not action for its own sake, but rather thoughtful efforts that are inspired by awareness and that mirror conscious choice. Through our endeavors we marshal our moxie to align our will with our intentions. And just as the radiance cast upon the Moon continues to grow during this lunar phase, the progress we make sheds light on our abilities, values, and desires.

The Invitation: Action

The First Quarter Moon is a time to take the steps necessary to significantly move your intention forward, even among obstacles that may arise. This lunar phase is a time for being in action, in which we experience catalyzing confrontations, navigate the crossroads, and have breakdowns and breakthroughs.

CATALYZING CONFRONTATIONS

During this lunar phase we may be confronted with challenges, hurdles we need to overcome. These confrontations may arise from within, as we try to align our beliefs and desires. Additionally, we may experience how our attachment to the past gets in the way of our vision for the future. While testing our resolve, working through any challenges that arise can help us to stretch and evolve.

The potential for confrontation may also exist between ourselves and others. As we're developing something new—whether a project or a perspective—we may find that it runs against the grain of someone else's vision. While this conflict may be irritating, it can result in our building more clarity and confidence, so that we can push forward rather than feel pulled back.

If we meet a constraint, we may sense that the only way out is through, and that what is needed for resolution is action rather than solely reflection. For example, let's say your project for the month involves reorganizing your kitchen. Instead of hemming and hawing about which cabinets the dishes, cookware, and serving pieces should go in, move them around and then imagine a few cooking scenarios to see whether their new location will make your food preparation more efficient and enjoyable.

Through a concentrated undertaking and the effort that it requires—whether relying solely upon our resources or in rallying the contributions of others—we can achieve great progress. We find ourselves connecting to a sense of freedom and a feeling of satisfaction that arises when we see how hard work can yield results, including how it can move our New Moon manifestations forward.

Infusing our actions with intention and thoughtfulness is really important at this time. If, instead, we find ourselves proceeding errantly, we may discover that we generate other obstacles that we will need to navigate. The actions that we take during this lunar phase may have us confronting and moving past our fears and the self-limiting stories we tell ourselves, and therefore become agents for catalyzing significant change.

 ## NAVIGATE THE CROSSROADS

As shared earlier, the First Quarter Moon brings us to a crossroads. We may feel that we're at a fork in the road, or perhaps several. Do we allow ghosts from our past to keep us stagnant or push through in the hope of dissolving them? Should we pursue a certain option or a different one? And importantly, do we move forward with our New Moon intention or just let it go? Having to navigate several potential

junctures is part of what gives this lunar phase the action-filled reputation that it has inherited.

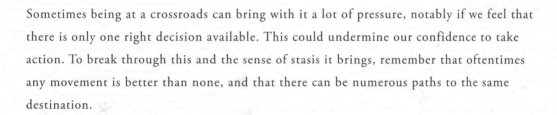

What are some strategies for doing so? First, just knowing that it's a time that emphasizes taking action and making decisions will allow you to not get caught off guard when you feel a significant need to do so. Also, while you may be busy juggling numerous proverbial plates, carve out a bit of quiet time so that you can remember not only what you wanted to create this month, but why—it can serve as an illuminating beacon at this moment.

Sometimes being at a crossroads can bring with it a lot of pressure, notably if we feel that there is only one right decision available. This could undermine our confidence to take action. To break through this and the sense of stasis it brings, remember that oftentimes any movement is better than none, and that there can be numerous paths to the same destination.

BREAKDOWNS AND BREAKTHROUGHS

As we act to forward our intentions and make choices at the crossroads, we begin to sense that we're at a turning point. As we sit at this spot, surveying the road ahead, we may have great breakthroughs. As we do things rather than just think about them, we gather lived experiences that offer us informative and inspirational *aha!* moments. At times we may find ourselves wanting to break from tradition, while at others we see the inherent intelligence of the traditional approaches upon which we often rely. We may experience breakthroughs in relationships, notably recognizing those that have us feeling limited or encumbered. If you find yourself faced with someone who is standing in your way, instead of just accepting that as your fate, see if there are any actions you can take to dissolve their opposition.

Tarot Reflections: The Lovers

The Lovers card embodies the period after the honeymoon is over, when the enchantment of what's new has receded and we are now face to face with the reality of what it is that we've embarked upon. While on first blush it would seem that the Lovers card is about romance, it's actually about choice in general. It signifies that we need to make an important decision in a relationship, whether it's one involving an alliance with another person or a project we've undertaken. This is similar to the First Quarter Moon: it's a moment in which we've reached a pivotal point of decision-making and in which we roll up our sleeves to do the work necessary to move forward. The Lovers card reminds us of the way through: to work on communicating honestly—not only with others but also ourselves—and to become really clear about what it is that we value. Knowing this will help you better choose which route you'll feel more consciously inclined to take and where your true commitments lie.

In addition to breakthroughs, breakdowns may be a theme, although this doesn't necessarily signify negative outcomes. For example, as we undertake actions, we may get a glimpse of structures that don't seem supportive of our vision or intention. It is these that we may witness falling apart, or for which we want to play an active role in their dismantling. And as we encounter resistance, a hallmark of the First Quarter Moon, we can both actively work to break through it as well as understand what it may be showing us.

While it's an active time, don't forget to take some breaks. Doing so will allow you to gain some distance from what you are doing so that you can see it with clearer eyes. Plus, it will help you temper the potential to be constantly on the move, which can be rather stressful. Being relaxed and feeling centered will pay off in spades in terms of the progress you can make during this lunar phase.

STELLAR REFLECTION QUESTIONS

Here are some journaling prompts to work with during the First Quarter Moon. They can help you navigate through this time with more clarity, further connecting to the insights and awareness that this lunar phase offers.

What turning points have I reached?

....

....

What actions am I taking to move my intention forward?

....

....

What criteria is guiding me in decision-making?

....

....

What tension am I facing?

....

....

What structures do I want to dismantle?

....

....

How am I navigating any conflicts I'm having with others?

....

....

Self-Care Activities

We can sequence our self-care efforts during the month to align with the opportunities, challenges, and stress patterns that may inherently arise during each lunar phase. Here are several activities to practice during the First Quarter Moon.

DANCE CLASS

In this lunar phase, we embrace being in motion. And when it comes to an activity that gets you moving and grooving, dance may be at the top of the list. Even if you don't consider yourself to have rhythm, muster up the courage to give it a whirl; after all, this is a period in which we're encouraged to take risks. See what piques your interest, whether it's learning salsa, hip-hop, ballroom, or another style. Opt to go solo or invite your partner or friend for an activity that's relationship-building. Check out offerings from fitness studios that offer dance-inspired exercise classes, a surefire way to have fun while getting a great cardiovascular workout. The First Quarter Moon is an invitation to stay bouncy so that we can bolster our ability to push through any roadblocks that emerge. And dance, as an activity centered on connecting to the beat and learning to pivot so that you can readily shift from one movement to another, can help you do just that.

PARTNER YOGA

Relationships play an important role in this lunar phase. We become more aware of who is an ally and who is an obstacle as we move forward with our New Moon intention. To help you feel more aligned with others, try partner yoga. By doing poses with another person, in this activity you not only see how they can help you stretch and strengthen, but you'll also enjoy an exercise that builds communication, trust, and problem-solving skills. While there are a multitude of poses to do, here are two to get you started. The first is a dual breathing practice in which you sit cross-legged facing each other, gently resting your hands on the other's knees. In tandem, take twenty deep breaths, feeling the flow of energy that exists between you. Another is a wide-seated leg stretch, in which you sit facing your partner with your legs outstretched to a V position, with your feet touching your partner's. Lean toward the other so that your palms are holding on to their forearms. As one person gently leans forward, the other leans back, giving you both a deep stretch in different areas. After six to eight breaths, come out of the pose and alternate who leans forward and who leans back.

WEIGHTED BLANKET

Resistance—and the pressure that it may engender—is a hallmark of this lunar phase. And while in the moment it could cause stress and uncertainty, in the act of pushing back against what we perceive to be a heavy weight, we may discover a solution that has both immediate and long-term benefits. A way to further tap into the experience of pressure— as well as its healing power—is pressure therapy, which involves the tactile sensation of feeling hugged or gently squeezed. One approach to do this is through the use of a weighted blanket. These duvets or throws contain heavy fill or are knitted using very dense yarn. When you place one on your body, it feels exceptionally comforting, like you're being cradled and held. Many people find that it offers them a deep sense of calm, helps quell anxiety, and relieves insomnia. If you find the gravity of the First Quarter Moon instills stress and you're looking for a way to invite in relaxation, try using a weighted blanket.

action items

- ◼ Take action.
- ◼ Have breakthroughs.
- ◼ Make decisions.
- ◼ Dismantle structures.
- ◼ Break from traditions.

- ◼ Take risks.
- ◼ Be agile.
- ◼ Discover allies.
- ◼ Resolve conflicts.
- ◼ Learn from resistance.

CHAPTER 5

GIBBOUS MOON

REFINEMENT

One look at the Gibbous Moon and you can sense a feeling of optimism. After all, not only is the majority of its visible surface beaming with light, but its incandescence continues to increase. Throughout this lunar phase, its illumination will grow until it transforms itself into the Full Moon, an inspirational icon that's been heralded in cultures throughout time.

It's not difficult, then, to see why we may feel infused with anticipation during the Gibbous Moon. We can deeply sense that we're on the verge of something grand, that a feeling of fulfillment is right around the corner. The atmosphere seems infused with a lot of promise. After all, given the location of the Gibbous Moon in the lunar cycle—much closer to its culmination than to its inception—our eyes are turned to the possibilities inherent in the future rather than the limitations we may have experienced in the past.

In the planting cycle, it is associated with the emergence of the bud, a symbol that reminds us that hope springs eternal. At this moment, we get a glimpse into the future and what is about to emerge, even if we don't necessarily know the exact shape and form it will take. Full clarity is yet to surface but we know it will soon arrive.

During the Gibbous Moon, we may find ourselves swelling with excitement and anticipation. And yet, we need to remember that while we are close to the blossoming of our New Moon intentions, we are not currently there. There is still time, and there is still work to be done. At this moment, we need to ensure that we don't allow anxious expectation and/or a sense of impatience to overtake us. If we do, we may find ourselves settling for a premature conclusion that stifles the promise of the vision we declared at the beginning of this lunar cycle.

Instead, use the opportunity inherent in the next few days to review what you've been manifesting, exploring what you have experienced and learned. From this vantage point, make adjustments to give further refinement to your creative venture. This will allow you to make the most of this final stretch of the waxing lunar period, an effort destined to give you further clarity when the Full Moon shines brightly in the sky.

The Invitation: Refinement

As the Gibbous Moon glows overhead, we enter a period in which we review and further polish what we've created. To orient effectively in this stage of refinement, we should watch out for a penchant for perfection, find new ways to galvanize trust, and follow a Goldilocks strategy, in which we're not doing too much or too little, but just the right amount.

A PENCHANT FOR PERFECTION

During the Gibbous Moon, we're called to refine our approach and make improvements. It's a time for self-development, in which we clearly recognize that we are in a process of evolving. With that, we feel pulled to take steps to better ourselves by learning new skills that will help us in our pursuit of conscious growth. This aspiration applies to whatever it is that we've been cultivating since the New Moon, as well as our life in general.

And while this can yield benefits and breakthroughs, we need to be careful that this hyper-focused lens toward improvement doesn't also bring with it too much pressure. After all, the drive to refine things may lead us down the path of wanting them to be perfect. But perfection is a bar that can never be reached and striving for it can have untoward effects, including worry, stress, and exhaustion. Additionally, it can catalyze excessive criticism, whether toward ourselves, others, or even the intention that has guided us over the last week-plus.

Instead of striving for perfection, embrace the action of perfecting. Put your energy behind doing things better rather than aiming for them to be the best. This will help you circumvent unnecessary stress and wasted hours for which you'll likely reap little reward. Additionally, it will leave you with more ease and a greater sense of freedom, both of which may enhance your ability to marshal your creativity at this moment. This can help

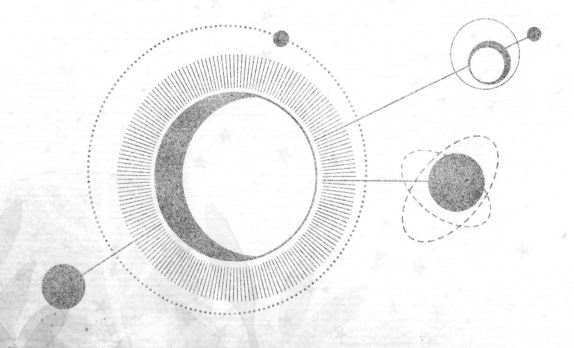

you not only polish your approaches but also better allocate your resources so that what you're building can further flourish.

GALVANIZE TRUST

One of the gifts that this period offers us is the ability to tap into a wellspring of faith in the process that we have undertaken and where it is leading us. It's built into the essence of this lunar phase. As we perceive so much of the Moon steeped in the Sun's rays, not only do we see it for what it is in the moment, but we have the innate sense of what follows: the complete illumination of the Full Moon.

And while we are still actively working on refining the structures we've been building, through tuning into our intuition we can discover a sense of flow that leads us to where we want to go. This can bolster our ability to trust ourselves and the way we orient to situations around us. As we reflect upon where we've been and where we're heading, we can tap into a deep sense of conviction that we are on the right path. We may come to realize that we have chosen our pursuits wisely and that whatever we will see at the Full Moon will be of value.

For example, let's say your aim during a given month is to feel more confident at work. During the Gibbous Moon, you may instinctively feel drawn to share an idea about a current project with a colleague. As they shower you with accolades for the value of your contribution, you realize that it's actually much easier than you had thought to express your opinions. Not only that: you get a glimpse of how feeling more self-assured not only puts you at ease but may also be a key to your creativity and productivity.

One of the factors that may enhance our sense of trust during this lunar phase is remembering that what we've been working on is not fully exposed and currently in view. Like the bud that is partially robed in the sepals that protect it, we may notice that we still feel shielded from some outer elements that can influence us. Part of what forms

Tarot Reflections: Strength

The Strength card is a beautiful representation of the Gibbous Moon. It reminds us that even if we're steeped in expectation and anticipation, we can access the patience to let things carry on at their own pace. It points to the virtue of allowing something to come into its own rather than forcing it. Strength invites us to get to know whatever it is that is gestating at the moment. Through doing so, we are able to make gentle adjustments that will resonate with our true essence and that of the creation that we are birthing. The card mirrors the legend of the *Beauty and the Beast*. In this tale, the maiden is innocent enough to befriend the ferocious creature, hopeful that with love and trust in the process of life's unfolding, he will surrender and be transformed. Magnificently, and in a testament to the power of acceptance—the cornerstone of Strength—he does.

our aegis is a bolstered ability to stay true to ourselves and our visions and values. What we may then discover is that, just as the sepal transforms from being protective to being supportive once the flower blossoms, our ability to further trust ourselves is an important ingredient in allowing us to flourish.

THE GOLDILOCKS OUTLOOK

The Gibbous Moon inspires us to propel forward, to continue building upon the structures that we have erected since the New Moon. With recognition that we're almost to the crest of this celestial cycle, just days away from the Full Moon, we may find ourselves instilled with enthusiasm and feeling really lit up. After all, just like the Moon, things feel pregnant with possibilities.

From this we can source the energy we need to take actions that can bring us to the finish line, those that not only allow us to feel more complete but also add additional luster to what we have been creating. We just need to be careful that any zealousness we can tap into doesn't have us overdo or overreach. Otherwise, we may find ourselves being spread too thin and lose sight of the end zone.

On the other hand, as we edge up to the Full Moon, we need to watch that we don't just rest on our laurels and stay static. It's a still a time when Luna's luminescence is increasing, so we should continue with actions at the behest of our original vision. Additionally, during this time, we need to watch out for the propensity to be impatient. After all the visioning and hard work we've put in recently, "Are we there yet?" could be a commonplace thought that incites irritability and/or has us wanting to sit out the rest of this active period and watch from the sidelines.

Adopt a Goldilocks outlook, trying to find the "just right"—that spot in between anticipation-inspired overenthusiasm and impatience-galvanized inactivity. Also, employ it to help you find a way to weave moments of restoration into this period of growth. This will allow you to discover the sweet spot in which your efforts are aligned, enabling you to be more confident in the action and orientation you undertake at this moment.

Self-Care Activities

We can sequence our self-care efforts during the month to align with the opportunities, challenges, and stress patterns that may inherently arise during each lunar phase. Here are several activities to practice during the Gibbous Moon.

MINDFULNESS

During the Gibbous Moon, we may find ourselves surveying a spectrum of details to see how they relate with one another. By doing so, we can then perceive what adjustments are called for so that we can improve and polish what we are working on. One way to fortify our ability to perceive things as clearly as possible—seeing them through fresh eyes rather than rote perspective—is by practicing mindfulness. Meditation is a great way to bolster a more mindful approach to life, and one that can be done in different ways. For example, you can sit or lie down, focusing on your breath, or you can opt to do a walking meditation in which you concentrate on your movements and bodily sensations. Additionally, meditation can be done inside or out in nature. Another contemplative practice is conscious eating, in which you eat in silence, chewing well and relishing each bite, while fully paying attention to the tastes, textures, and aromas you experience. Even if you already practice one of these activities, see if spending more time doing it during this lunar phase helps you to experience the blooming of a greater level of awareness.

 ## MASSAGE

As you focus on propelling your intentions and goals forward, it's quite an active time, one where you're likely to be on the move a lot. If all the hustle is causing a lot of bustle that's exacerbating tension, take a time-out and treat yourself to a massage. There are many types from which to choose. The most popular form, known as Swedish massage, offers a gentle treatment in which the massage therapist uses gliding strokes to work through muscular tension and increase blood circulation. Deep-tissue massage, like its name implies, targets the inner layers of muscles and connective tissues through the application of more sustained pressure. It is often used therapeutically for pain release and injury healing. And then there's chair massage, which offers a quicker and less expensive approach that focuses upon your neck, head, and shoulders. Regardless of the style you choose, you'll experience an array of benefits: not only can massage help to reduce stress and tension, but it will also leave you feeling relaxed and refreshed, ready to take on the next activity on your Gibbous Moon to-do list.

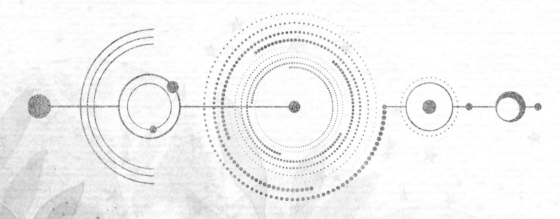

STELLAR REFLECTION QUESTIONS

Here are some journaling prompts to work with during the Gibbous Moon.
They can help you navigate through this time with more clarity, further
connecting to the insights and awareness that this lunar phase offers.

What am I really excited about?

....

....

What adjustments need to be made to further hone the project I'm
working on?

....

....

What possibilities feel really alive right now?

....

....

How can I make things better without feeling the need to have them be perfect?

....

....

What strategies can I employ to temper any impatience I'm currently feeling?

....

....

What gets in my way of trusting myself?

....

....

MEAL PLANNING

In this lunar phase, we take a step back to see the whole picture so that we can view where we currently are and where we want to go. When it comes to your self-care regimen, one way to honor the invitation to cast a broad view and allow it to help you refine your movement forward is meal planning, an activity aligned with this time. Whether it's for the entirety of this lunar phase or longer, you begin at the same starting point: first look in your refrigerator, freezer, and pantry to see what's there that needs to be consumed in the coming days. Then think about the types of meals you may be interested in eating. Considering this, survey cookbooks, websites, and foodie friends to find recipes that appeal to you. Sketch out your meal calendar, make a shopping list, purchase the food, and then do any prep work necessary for all the meals. While it seems like a lot of work at the front end, it will not only save you time and money over the course of days, but it will be easier to cook food that you really enjoy.

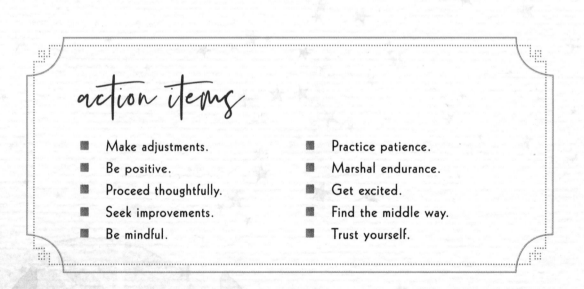

action items

- Make adjustments.
- Be positive.
- Proceed thoughtfully.
- Seek improvements.
- Be mindful.

- Practice patience.
- Marshal endurance.
- Get excited.
- Find the middle way.
- Trust yourself.

CHAPTER 6

FULL MOON

ILLUMINATION

Imagine your ancestors centuries ago, before the invention of artificial light, before streetlamps cast their hue upon neighborhoods and incandescent light bulbs allowed homes to glow no matter the hour. Back then, activities and outings were concentrated during the day, because when night arrived, the sky was dark and the environment stygian.

Yet, one time each month, a fully illuminated beacon arose overhead, lighting the path for all, allowing people to gather, hunt, convene, and roam with the greater ease that comes from clearer vision. It became a prized moment infused with reverence, a cause for celebration hallowed with significance. It was the moment of the Full Moon.

When something is full, it contains or holds as much as it possibly can. In the case of the Moon, we experience it as replete with luminosity. During this lunar phase, barring cloud cover, the entirety of our day features a sky-bound light—the Sun radiates it directly during the daytime and the Moon fully reflects the solar rays to us during the nighttime.

At the peak of the Full Moon, its brightness cannot be overstated: while you may think that it would be twice as bright as the First or Last Quarter Moon—in which half of the Moon's visible surface is filled with light—it's actually between six and fifteen times brighter.

Of all the Moon phases, this is the one that most captures our attention and has become a symbol shared across the globe of power, potential, fruition, and guidance. A combination of mystical allure and practical value, with this luminescence aloft, the Full Moon holds eternal sway in the imaginations, legends, and arts of cultures around the world. Its significance is such that the timing of many important holidays is based upon it. For example, Easter occurs on the first Sunday after the Full Moon following the March Equinox. And one of the most celebrated holidays in Chinese culture, the Moon Festival, occurs each year on the Full Moon in late September or early October.

Every Full Moon feels like an enchanting event. As we see Luna bathed in solar light, we too feel lit up. We sense a deeper connection between ourselves and the world around us, as we imagine others across the globe seeing what we see and being inspired by this lunar radiance. As our path is illuminated and we experience something coming into its full being, we become present to the inherent awe, promise, and hope that life offers.

The Invitation: Illumination

As we arrive at the Full Moon, we find ourselves at a moment filled with clearer vision. We harness the potential this phase has for illumination through watching for the emergence of clarity, recognizing the power of shadows, and knowing that it's a period of heightened emotionality.

EMERGENT CLARITY

During the Full Moon, a brightness beckons and the clarity that we were hoping for appears. What were once seeds of intention and vision, planted weeks ago when the lunar cycle began, have now become flowers. What was recently just potential has now become manifest. We get more exact glimpses of the shapes and forms that are emerging.

During this time, we begin to see the results of the actions recently taken. What occurs may just as likely be inner lucidity as it is awareness about something external to us. For example, in addition to experiencing our project coming to fruition, we may find ourselves having *aha!* moments that inform how we think or feel about an issue or situation. If we are delighted with what has come into being, we may find ourselves reveling in a sense of accomplishment. We beam with radiance in having broken new ground or having experienced a breakthrough in how we perceive things.

However, Full Moons can be an equal-opportunity spotlight, highlighting weaknesses just as they do strengths. For example, if we've cut corners as we've embarked upon our initiative, it's these limitations—or their consequences—that may come to light. Or, if our presumptions about something or someone were built on shaky ground, we may now experience the associated ramifications. What then gains luminosity is not joy but possibly upset and disappointment. This may be one of the reasons that some think of Full Moons as periods with the potential for augmented stress.

Whether it seems like you're reaping payoffs or penalties at this phase, it's important to recall—as the lunar cycle reminds us—that nothing is static and that everything evolves. The Full Moon, after all, is a very powerful pivot point: just as the Moon's perceived light reaches its capacity, it shifts into the waning phase, and its light begins to recede. As you gather awareness at this moment, remember that it's possible to embark upon course-correction strategies in the coming days.

SHADOW RECOGNITION

One of the many lessons of the lunar cycle is how light and dark are inextricably intertwined. For example, an integral ingredient in the formation of shadows is light. When an object obstructs the path of luminescence, a dark silhouette is created. Given that they are products of illumination, it seems that shadows—in particular, our personal shadows—can serve as *prima materia* during this time to help us access a greater spectrum of clarity.

Dealing with Setbacks

If you feel that what you set about to accomplish at the New Moon hasn't succeeded, don't dismay. There is still more work that you can do during the next two lunar phases. And if it still needs more time and effort, you can take your intention and renew it at a subsequent New Moon, using the great awareness you gained during these weeks to help it develop into its full potential.

Lunar Eclipses

Lunar Eclipses are associated with Full Moons, with these lunations occurring up to three times a year. From an astrology perspective, it's thought that what they bring to light may have even more awareness-shifting potential than monthly Full Moons. Therefore, during the time of a Lunar Eclipse, pay attention to what you notice to see if the illumination you receive has even more gravity than usual.

What are our personal shadows? According to Jungian psychology, the shadow is that part of ourselves from which we keep distance, the aspects of our personality we deem hard to accept or view as inappropriate, or with which we don't readily identify. Our shadow side may include our repressed thoughts and feelings, those that we've disowned due to societal conditioning.

So, if we consider Full Moons to be a time when our shadows may be activated, we can then be on the lookout for them as signposts for understanding. Finding yourself overly bothered by someone? Feeling especially conflicted, even about how your New Moon intention has manifested? Noticing that you're a bit more triggered than normal? If so, honestly probe to see whether it's any of the usual shadow suspects—fear, shame, jealousy, desire, guilt, or unworthiness—that underlies your aggravation.

If the answer is a resounding *yes*, or even a lukewarm *maybe*, take note. Sure, doing so may feel a bit sticky—there's a reason we banish these feelings to the basement of our consciousness, after all. However, consider what was just illuminated and the breakthrough in awareness you received to be a treasure. Continuing to bring it to light—acknowledging and integrating it—will grant you more clarity about your thoughts, feelings, and motivations. It can lead to a greater sense of freedom and an enhanced ability to more consciously express the whole of who you are. This has an array of benefits, of course, not the least of which is gaining more awareness about your New Moon intention and how it's manifesting. For some shadow work suggestions, see page 73.

 ## HEIGHTENED EMOTIONALITY

It now likely makes more sense why Full Moons are thought to be a time of heightened emotionality. With this lunation bringing clarity—whether of something wonderful, or something that's left us wondering—we can't help but have feelings emerge. Just thinking of how Luna, a symbol for our emotional reservoir, appears to be under the spotlight during this lunation, it should be no surprise that our moods, like the tides, may be swayed during a Full Moon.

Another reason for heightened emotionality during this time can be understood if we look to the dynamics of the Full Moon itself, which occurs when the Sun and Moon stand diametric to each other with the Earth in the center. From an astrological perspective, during this lunation the Sun and Moon occupy zodiac signs opposite each other; with that, potential conflict can arise as we feel pulled between two seemingly contrary options

Tarot Reflections: Temperance

Temperance is the card of alchemy, reflecting the integration of opposites and the powerful awareness that emerges in the process. This beautifully mirrors the Full Moon, whose hallmark illumination is the result of the Sun and Moon residing on opposing sides of the zodiacal landscape. Through Temperance, we are called to appreciate the light and the dark, the rational and emotional, and the alchemical marriage of the masculine and feminine. It reminds us of the power of not only holding the tension of contrasting forces but also of balancing and synthesizing them. In doing so, we can turn lead into gold, and realize the potential of our creative energies. Temperance reflects an experience or moment like the Full Moon: filled with opportunities for growth. When you pull this card, it also represents the importance of unearthing heightened emotions and how that is an essential part of the art of learning.

or modes of expression. Until we reach a resolution, we may find ourselves with rising stress levels. This may undermine our resilience and ability to consciously express our feelings.

A way to sidestep some, if not all, of this stress? First, just knowing that sensitivity abounds during these days can help you be in rhythm with the moment, rather than being caught off guard by a stream of feelings you didn't expect. Additionally, it's important to realize that it's a period in which we're being invited to perceive polarities while trying to weave together a synthesized understanding. By finding the relationship that exists between different inputs, we can discover a way that they can symbiotically exist. We can see the beauty of this orientation rather than finding ourselves in the habit of opting for one approach and then banishing the other. We honor both sides of each proverbial coin and realize the value of doing so. And with that, we not only behold otherwise uncharted solutions but may find a way that helps us avoid excess disquietude.

STELLAR REFLECTION QUESTIONS

Here are some journaling prompts to work with during the Full Moon. They can help you navigate through this time with more clarity, further connecting to the insights and awareness that this lunar phase offers.

In what ways have my New Moon intentions come to light?

....

....

What's the source of any gratification I'm experiencing?

....

....

What is at the root of any disappointment I'm experiencing?

....

....

When I'm overwhelmed by my emotions, how is it that I best take care of myself?

....

....

What conflicts am I noticing and how am I resolving them?

....

....

If I'm finding myself especially triggered, what's the catalyst?

....

....

Self-Care Activities

We can sequence our self-care efforts during the month to align with the opportunities, challenges, and stress patterns that may inherently arise during each lunar phase. Here are several activities to practice during the Full Moon.

MOON BATHING

During the Full Moon, bathe in the light of the night sky. Weather permitting, go for walks or even do a picnic dinner outdoors. Look to the Moon, feeling inspired by the lunar light as you imagine you're absorbing it. As you do, connect to your inner wild child, whose presence you may strongly feel these days, and even let yourself howl at the Moon and see how it energizes you. Also, schedule time for a Luna-inspired evening bath: fill the tub with hot water, mineral salts, your favorite essential oils, and some Moon water. How to make Moon water? The night before, place some filtered water in a glass bowl (with your favorite crystals if you'd like) and leave it outside for several hours, allowing it to absorb the luminescence of the Moon. If you don't have a tub, don't worry. Instead, do a foot bath with Moon water. You can also take this aqueous elixir and place it in a mister bottle, using it as a refreshing facial toner or room spray.

SLEEP SANCTIFICATION

Many people notice that their sleep is more fitful on Full Moon nights; perhaps you've found this to be the case for you, too. In fact, Full Moons have been associated with a slight increase in how long it takes people to fall asleep as well as a marginal reduction in the amount of sleep they get. Both of these factors have been linked to greater morning fatigue. While focusing on your sleep quality is important throughout the month, if you can only dedicate several days to a sleep-sanctification practice, do it during the Full Moon. Get into bed at least thirty minutes earlier than usual. Before doing so, carve out time to wind down—practicing relaxing yoga poses, enjoying your favorite cup of herbal tea, and/or doing some calming breathing exercises. When in bed, allow yourself to survey the day, connecting to several things for which you are grateful, as this can inspire calm and may lull you to sleep.

SHADOW WORK

To gather further clarity at the Full Moon, do a shadow work exercise. First, sit quietly for several minutes, closing your eyes and breathing rhythmically to center yourself. Then, focus upon someone that you find rattling. Envision that person in your mind's eye and connect to their words or behaviors that you experience as provoking. As you do that, ask yourself whether they are somehow serving as a mirror for you, and whether any of their triggering traits are those that you see (although often cover up) within yourself. If you discover that any of their expressed qualities actually resonate within you, write that down in your journal. Over time, continue to reflect upon whether this is an aspect of yourself that you find hard to accept. As you do, be compassionate with yourself as this can be challenging work. However, remind yourself that it's worth it, as owning both our light and our dark is key to healing and living our lives from a place of awareness.

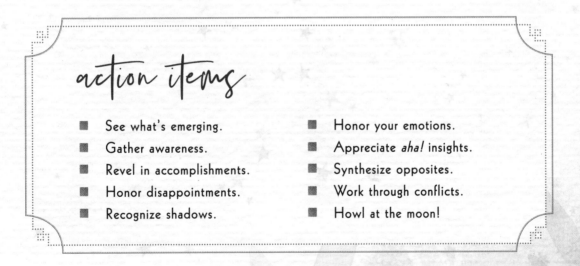

action items

- See what's emerging.
- Gather awareness.
- Revel in accomplishments.
- Honor disappointments.
- Recognize shadows.
- Honor your emotions.
- Appreciate *aha!* insights.
- Synthesize opposites.
- Work through conflicts.
- Howl at the moon!

CHAPTER 7

DISSEMINATING MOON

SHARING

The Disseminating Moon follows on the heels of the Full Moon, Luna's peak period of illumination. In this phase—also referred to as Waning Gibbous—the Moon is still infused with an abundance of light. The term *gibbous* signifies something swollen; one look at the Moon at this moment, with its apparent bulging shape, gives testament to its name. If this term sounds familiar it's because, as you may remember, the phase preceding the Full Moon is known as Gibbous (see page 56). As that one occurred in the waxing period, its radiance increased over time. During this one, its visible light diminishes as the days pass.

When viewed symbolically, during this lunar phase the light of the Moon is not something perceived to be lost but rather shared, as its name—*disseminating*—implies. It's no wonder then that the Disseminating Moon is a time known for communicating, broadcasting, and publishing ideas, including those that came to light during the Full Moon. As Luna sheds her light, we receive a powerful opportunity to shed light on what we've learned. The relationship orientation of the Disseminating Moon can also be appreciated when we reflect upon how this lunar phase is the one that corresponds to the planting stage in which bees are drawn to the flower for pollination.

An inherent sense of goodwill and sociability marks this period. We're motivated to communicate our thoughts with others because we inherently sense that what we've learned will be of benefit to them. All the while, we also feel that doing so will be a boon for us, by helping us to further integrate and assimilate what we've experienced.

With its sharing and convivial nature, it's easy to see how the Disseminating Moon phase has been traditionally connected with Lammas, the neo-pagan holiday associated with the harvest. It and other celebratory festivals throughout the world—including the Rice Harvest Festival in Bali, Vendimia in Argentina, and Olivagando in Italy—feature the coming together of the community to gather, reconnect, and celebrate in honor of the harvest. This lunar phase captures this spirit, being a socially oriented time of communing and communicating, and sharing the fruits of our labor.

The Invitation: Sharing

As the Disseminating Moon appears, there's an inspiration to take what we've learned and broadcast it to those around us. As we're focused upon sharing, it's a period that invites us to spread the word, foster community connections, and embrace a desire to give.

SPREADING THE WORD

You've got wisdom to share and now feels like an engaging time to convey it. You've learned a lot over the last weeks, including seeing how your New Moon intentions have taken shape and form. And whether you're basking in your success or feeling disappointed by things that have recently occurred, there's likely a rash of thoughts and feelings bubbling up within you now, which you're feeling called to share. There's a sense that what you've learned not only has value for you but can also be an asset for others. To that aim, you may find yourself wanting to ring up a relative, schedule a meeting with a colleague, or gather with friends to relay important insights.

Not only can others learn a lot from you, but you can learn a lot from sharing your insights with them. Having someone witness and hold space for you as you communicate your ideas and sentiments will allow you to further synthesize what you know.

It's not just you who wants to communicate right now—it's actually the activity du jour these days. As such, you may find yourself exposed to information overload. To make sure to keep centered and stay focused, build in opportunities for a little solitude during this relatively social period. Weaving in a bit of contemplative time will also help you further distill all that you've been learning. Even short stints of quiet can allow for the awareness that resides deep within to surface and be disseminated to your conscious mind.

What's powerful about these days is that communication is not just limited to the personal. If other factors align, the Disseminating Moon is thought to be an auspicious time to broadcast a message to the community at large. Whether it's the launch of a website, the circulating of a press release, the initiation of a marketing campaign, or the like, your dispatch may discover an audience more amenable to being educated at this time.

COMMUNITY CONNECTIONS

As noted previously, part of what drives our propensity for wanting to communicate during the Disseminating Moon is a desire to share knowledge with others for their benefit. Coupling the generosity that may underlie this with a heightened desire to meet and greet can have us primed to connect with our crew and gather together over these days. As such, it's not surprising that this lunar phase is thought to be one in which our interest in being social is stimulated. Sure, there may be times when you want to soak in some private time. However, on the whole, it's not a period that champions solely being siloed or separated. Instead, honor an elevated desire for fellowship and camaraderie.

If the Full Moon awarded you with triumphs, you'll want to celebrate. Whether you plan a special outing or rendezvous on a video call, make time to commune with your BFFs. Even if your recent experiences had more fizzle than sparkle, you may still find yourself heeding the clarion call to commune with others. After all, you know how, time and time again, your trusted friends can help you make lemonade from any lemons you've encountered.

It's not just intimate events that feel aligned during this period, but any that involve the gathering of people who want to partake in their shared interests. Just like the harvest festivals in which the community comes together to celebrate the fruits of their labor, it's a powerful time to convene. As such, during this lunar phase, you may find yourself more inclined to participate in a community project, go to a play, or be involved in a fundraiser. Planning a conference or workshop where people can learn, seek advice, and/or exchange viewpoints? If the timing aligns, consider the Disseminating Moon when you set out to schedule it.

 ## A DESIRE TO GIVE

The Disseminating Moon is a time that feels imbued with generosity. After all, we take what we've collected and gift it to others, rather than just keeping it for ourselves. We're inclined to offer our insights, lessons learned from lived experiences, and perspectives on topics that matter to us. And with that, we may seek an audience to whom we can bestow our feelings, thoughts, and ideas.

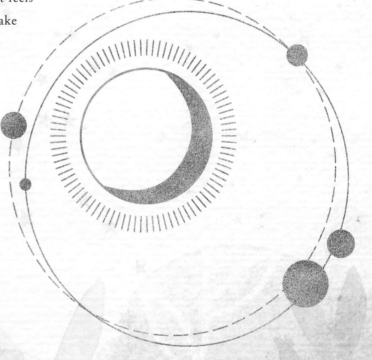

There's a sense of bounty, and a heightened willingness to give of ourselves. In fact, you may notice that you want to contribute more than you

Tarot Reflections: The Hierophant

To understand more about the Disseminating Moon, we can look to the tarot card of the Hierophant. Reflecting the archetype of the spiritual teacher, the Hierophant embodies higher wisdom. It captures the essence of wanting to give voice to what you know and the desire to share that knowledge with others. It represents a partnership between what is above and what is below—including our conscious and subconscious minds—which can bolster our ability to inhabit soulful sagacity. This card reflects a generosity of spirit and the desire to spread the word, notably to a like-minded community, just as is called for during the Disseminating Moon. Similar to the Hierophant, during this lunar phase we don't just share out of responsibility, but we carry an intentional enthusiasm to do so. If we look to the roots of the word *enthusiasm*, we see that *en* signifies "in" and *theos* means "the divine." This is another way of seeing how this lunar phase is aligned with the Hierophant and its sanctified qualities.

usually do, or that others are doing the same. As this period, though, can be a time when overenthusiasm holds sway, watch that you don't pledge more than you want or are able to deliver.

A desire to more actively distribute what we possess may also inspire a heightened charitability during this period. And with this, tithing may be a theme. While traditionally thought of as allocating a portion (usually a tenth) of one's earnings in support of a religious organization, the amount and beneficiary of tithings can vary. If you're feeling a philanthropic wave during this lunar phase, donate some money—whether to a favorite charity or someone in need. Remember, though, that tithing doesn't have to be limited to financial offerings: you can just as well share of yourself through altruistic acts, volunteering your time to an organization you care about or participating in a justice-promoting civic action.

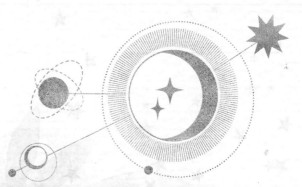

STELLAR REFLECTION QUESTIONS

Here are some journaling prompts to work with during the Disseminating Moon. They can help you navigate through this time with more clarity, further connecting to the insights and awareness that this lunar phase offers.

With whom do I want to share my Full Moon realizations, and why?

....

....

What message am I ready to broadcast?

....

....

What am I really enthusiastic about at the moment?

....

....

Who would best benefit from my generosity right now?

....

....

To whom do I feel really grateful?

....

....

What activities best help me to relax and center my mind?

....

....

Self-Care Activities

We can sequence our self-care efforts during the month to align with the opportunities, challenges, and stress patterns that may inherently arise during each lunar phase. Here are several activities to practice during the Disseminating Moon.

GRATITUDE PRACTICE

The Disseminating Moon is a period in which we may find ourselves brimming with gratitude for experiences we've recently had, the people who guided us on our path, and/or life in general. As such, a gratitude practice feels like a very aligned activity for these times. It's something quite simple to do, which you can approach in numerous ways. Each morning or evening you can dedicate time to writing in your journal, noting the things and people for which you are grateful. Another idea is to send a thank-you note to someone who has offered you valuable support. Additionally, you could make the focus of your meditation something for which you are greatly appreciative, allowing it to both center and nourish you. Not only is connecting to gratitude a way to channel the energies of these days, but it will provide you with important long-standing benefits. Research has shown that those who actively cultivate it are happier and more optimistic, and that it is a key to building healthy relationships.

GROUP ACTIVITIES

The Disseminating Moon is a socially oriented time, one in which we gain pleasure and tap into a sense of possibility through enjoying the company of others. Knowing this, one way to augment your commitment to self-care during these days is to participate in group activities. Instead of going it alone exercising, partake in a fitness class, whether in person or online. Or call up a friend and invite them to go on a walk or run with you; not only will this motivate you both to cover more ground, but you may find it to be a great opportunity to catch up and share recent experiences. If you're looking for information on a particular dietary supplement, relaxation practice, or cooking technique, instead of researching it on the Web, ring up several people you trust to get their advice and recommendations. Given the lunar phase you're in, they will likely be more than happy to share what they know.

SOUND HEALING

Given the propensity for communication these days offer, you may find it helpful to carve out a little time free from conversation. In addition to periods of sheer quiet, consider the healing balm of sound. The first place to start is surrounding yourself with music. Listening to tunes—whether while working, driving, or out for a run—can not only focus your mind but inspire your heart. It's also a creative time to make a playlist: tune in to your New Moon intention and all that's been manifesting from it and compile a series of songs that evoke its theme and mission. Additionally, you can also enjoy some sound therapy practices. Find a bodywork therapist who uses special tuning forks calibrated to specific vibrations, applying them to acupuncture points to create more energy flow. Another idea is to attend a sound bath, whether in person or online. The facilitators of these classes help invoke a meditative state using ambient sounds from singing bowls or gongs.

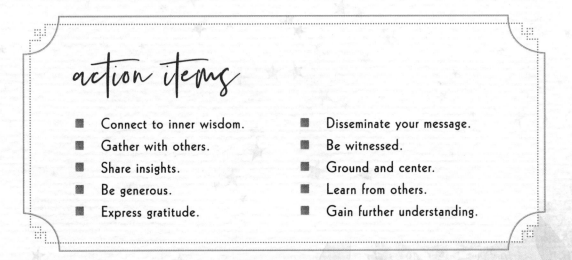

action items

- Connect to inner wisdom.
- Gather with others.
- Share insights.
- Be generous.
- Express gratitude.
- Disseminate your message.
- Be witnessed.
- Ground and center.
- Learn from others.
- Gain further understanding.

CHAPTER 8

LAST QUARTER MOON

MATURITY

The Last Quarter Moon marks a significant moment. It heralds a pivotal juncture, as we are midway between the vivid illumination of the Full Moon and the supreme darkness of the New Moon. As it begins, it forges a commanding image: the light and dark on its visible surface are evenly balanced.

We can see the light and dark as partners, existing in a symbolic marriage of equality. We can also just as readily imagine a poetic tension that exists where they meet, seeing them as pushing against the other and creating friction. And with that, we can perceive a sense of resistance and pressure, which are hallmarks of this lunar phase. Yet, during these days, we need not get overwhelmed by tension. Instead, we should see how any emergent conflict that arises can push us to new levels of consciousness, encouraging us to take actions that can bring projects to a whole new level of success.

As the Last Quarter Moon proceeds, the striking image that we associated with this lunar phase begins to morph as the Moon loses more light, heading to the completion of this current lunar cycle. This reminds us of the impermanence of even the most iconic of structures, inherently connecting us to another theme highlighted in this phase: during these days we become present to how breakdowns can lead to breakthroughs. It's a time in which we also need to make adjustments, with some of our adaptations involving releasing and letting go, just like the Moon is doing with its light.

Being closer to the end of the lunar cycle rather than the beginning could instill us with concern and stress. We may find ourselves connecting to a disconcerting feeling, best embodied in the German word *torschlusspanik*—the fear that time is running out. While time pressure may abound, remember to just do the best you can in the moments you have.

We may also experience a bit of impatience, ready to move on from what we've been working on for the past three-plus weeks. Additionally, we may be sensing that we're on the verge of reaching the finish line. Despite the resistance we may feel, it's important to undertake the conscious action and movement that this period calls for so that we can experience a sense of completion of what we envisioned at the New Moon.

The Invitation: Maturity

As the Last Quarter Moon shines in the sky, we find the persistence to push through tension, taking action that brings us to a more holistic sense of completion. In this phase in which we see how our projects are reaching a greater level of maturity, we become aware of how being accountable yields great reward, that resistance can be transformative, and how less is often more.

ACCOUNTABILITY

Things really come together at the Last Quarter Moon. We witnessed our intentions coming to life at the Full Moon, and further understood their import through getting feedback during the Disseminating Moon. And now here we are at a lunar phase in which we can take what we've learned and make final adjustments. Whether we are thrilled or disappointed by what has recently come to pass, it's a time to step up to the plate in a final push to see our vision through.

Being accountable—to ourselves and others—is a key invitation of this time. Maturity is heralded as we find ourselves needing to accept responsibility for the choices we've made. We may find ourselves overrun with obligations, some necessary to tie up loose ends to find a sense of completion to something we initiated weeks ago. And yet as much as this may have us feeling a sense of overwhelm, if we answer the call of what needs our attention, we can discover the resilience to weather any storm.

The structures we may rely on are also held accountable during this period, whether they are our routines, beliefs, relationships, or the institutions with which we are involved. And with that, there may be times when we see how these have outworn their usefulness, and that we need to let them go to make space for new ones to emerge. If you experience breakdowns, even among any shock or stress you experience, see how this may eventually lead to transformative breakthroughs. Take a few moments to look back over the past few weeks and inventory what worked really well for you and what didn't. This type of accounting will pay off in spades for your future endeavors.

VIVE LA RÉSISTANCE

Like the Moon—divided in two halves, one light and one dark—we too may find ourselves holding contradictions during this time. And feeling ourselves at the midway point, equally positioned between the Full Moon and New Moon, we could feel a bit betwixt and between the past and future.

An arising sense of tension could make us feel edgy. For example, just as we perceive we're close to our project's finish line, we may find ourselves bored or disengaged, and just want to call it a day. All the while, we may

realize—perhaps bemoaningly—that there is more work to be done, more action that we need to take. A feeling of strife could also arise if we know in our heart of hearts that we need to let go of something while also feeling attached to it, making it difficult to do so.

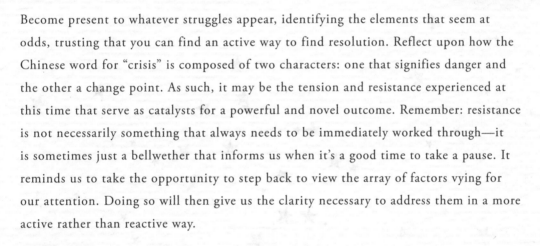

The resistance we feel may be from within us or we may meet it in obstacles along our path. While it may seem chafing, the resistance can push us to grow by motivating us to figure out the adjustments necessary for things to proceed in the most integrated way. Remember that resistance literally builds muscles by making them work against an opposing force.

Become present to whatever struggles appear, identifying the elements that seem at odds, trusting that you can find an active way to find resolution. Reflect upon how the Chinese word for "crisis" is composed of two characters: one that signifies danger and the other a change point. As such, it may be the tension and resistance experienced at this time that serve as catalysts for a powerful and novel outcome. Remember: resistance is not necessarily something that always needs to be immediately worked through—it is sometimes just a bellwether that informs us when it's a good time to take a pause. It reminds us to take the opportunity to step back to view the array of factors vying for our attention. Doing so will then give us the clarity necessary to address them in a more active rather than reactive way.

 ## LESS IS MORE

No matter how present we are to the opportunities and challenges of the current moment, we inherently sense that a fresh start—in the form of the upcoming new lunar cycle—is closer than further away. And with that, while we are still actively engaged in refining what we've been creating, we also intuit the need to release that which is outworn. Just as Luna is relinquishing its light, we too are called to let go of involvements and attitudes that are past their prime. The theme of *less is more* and its relation to fresh starts is inherently reflected in the planting stage that corresponds with the Third Quarter Moon: it's when the fruit is harvested, or, if left on the plant, begins to decay, beginning the

Tarot Reflections: The World

The World reminds us of the importance of accountability and conscientiousness, qualities emphasized during the Last Quarter Moon. Through this card, we further realize that we need to be responsible: for ourselves, for what we create, and for doing the work required to build a world in which we would like to live. It carries with it a knowledge of the resistance that exists when we witness polarities, while also signaling that magnificent outcomes can arise if we bring opposites together harmoniously. The World is the final card of the major arcana. And while the Last Quarter is not the final lunar phase, it is the last one in which we do concerted shepherding of our New Moon intentions. When we pull this card, it signifies that we're in the final push to bring things to fruition. As we work diligently, we do so while embodying a deep sense of empowerment. It carries with it the essence of maturity and a sense of completion, just like the Last Quarter Moon.

process that will subsequently lead to releasing its seed back to the earth.

Apply the less-is-more principle to the project or new chapter you've been working on over the past three weeks, seeing how pruning something can actually give the creation more strength and integrity. For example, let's say that your New Moon intention centered on getting in shape, and for this aim, you embarked upon working out six days a week. Now, here at this moment, you find yourself tense and exhausted. This may have you realize that you've been overdoing it and that scaling back to five days will actually get you where you want to be faster.

Let's reflect upon another example. Imagine that your goal this month was to rekindle a certain friendship, and that after concerted attempts to do so, all that you've received is stress and uneasiness. In this case, it may be the whole intention of reigniting the relationship that needs to be released. Along with that, what you may let go of is the years' worth of second-guessing yourself as to whether you initially made the right call to dissolve the relationship in the first place.

STELLAR REFLECTION QUESTIONS

Here are some journaling prompts to work with during the Last Quarter Moon. They can help you navigate through this time with more clarity, further connecting to the insights and awareness that this lunar phase offers.

What final push do I need to make to manifest my New Moon intention?

....

....

What needs to be pruned?

....

....

How are breakdowns leading to breakthroughs?

....

....

Where am I noticing both internal and external resistance?

....

....

What conflicts am I experiencing, and what are they showing me?

....

....

What have I noticed is past its prime?

....

....

The call for surrender and release, of course, may not just be limited to something under the auspices of your New Moon intention. For instance, it's also the time to clear away outworn attitudes, release bad habits, and cut the cord with belief systems that hold you back. On a practical level, it offers the invitation to let things go as well: purge your closets, clear away clutter, and throw out expired foods from your refrigerator. Not only will you feel a sense of liberation, but you'll be making space for the new that will arrive soon.

Self-Care Activities

We can sequence our self-care efforts during the month to align with the opportunities, challenges, and stress patterns that may inherently arise during each lunar phase. Here are several activities to practice during the Last Quarter Moon.

EXFOLIATE YOUR SKIN

Given that the Last Quarter Moon is a time to cast off what's outworn, if you don't already do so regularly, take the time to exfoliate your skin. It can help boost cell turnover, giving your skin a great glow and heightened ability to absorb moisture. For a skin-softening body treatment, use an exfoliating brush, mitt, or cloth to slough away dead skin cells while showering or bathing. Or opt for a scrub made from sugar or salt, which you can easily make at home. When it comes to your face, numerous approaches abound: you could opt for a serum made with either alpha- or beta-hydroxy acids; a cleanser featuring finely granulated ingredients such as brown rice, bamboo, or rosehip seeds; or use a linen washcloth for mechanical exfoliation. Remember, though, to be gentle in your approach, as a heavy hand could lead to redness and inflammation.

DIGITAL DETOX

The Last Quarter Moon is a period in which we align with a less-is-more orientation. As such, consider making it a monthly time to do a digital detox, reducing the time you spend online. Doing so is not only a great stress-reduction strategy but will make space for more relaxing analog activities. There are numerous ways to disconnect from your devices without going cold turkey with your tech gadgets for this whole lunar phase. For example, instead of checking email in bed upon arising, wait to survey your inbox while enjoying your morning coffee. Additionally, unless you're in the midst of a research project, close your browser so that you won't feel compelled to check the news or your favorite entertainment site. To invite more restful sleep and avoid the pull to doom scroll before bed, keep your phone somewhere other than your nightstand. Also, take a break from social media for a day or longer, giving yourself a hiatus from an activity that may not only undermine productivity but also stir up feelings of anxiety.

 ## RESISTANCE EXERCISE

As shared earlier, resistance is one of the hallmark experiences of the Last Quarter Moon. And while it may bring us tension at times, it also can have numerous benefits, including for our well-being. For example, resistance training has been found to not only strengthen muscle but also bones, ligaments, and tendons. Of course, this type of exercise should be an integrated part of any fitness program and not just practiced during one period each month; however, if you've left it out of your workouts for a while, this may be a time to pick it back up again or dedicate additional time to practicing it. For example, take a break from computer time to do several squats, lunges, and/or push-ups. Also, do a few rounds of plank pose, working your way up to holding it for sixty seconds at a time. If you'd like to shake up your workouts and try different types of approaches, find a strength-training class online or at your gym that incorporates resistance bands, weights, or kettlebells.

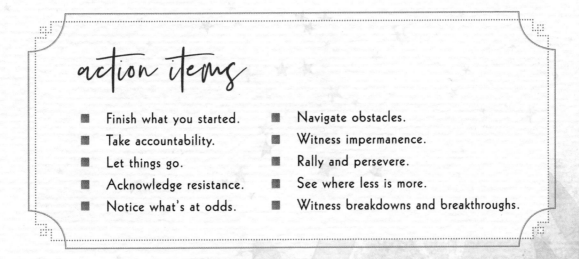

action items

- Finish what you started.
- Take accountability.
- Let things go.
- Acknowledge resistance.
- Notice what's at odds.
- Navigate obstacles.
- Witness impermanence.
- Rally and persevere.
- See where less is more.
- Witness breakdowns and breakthroughs.

CHAPTER 9

BALSAMIC MOON

RENEWAL

Like the New Moon, the Balsamic Moon is a time when Luna is veiled in darkness. Yet during this lunar phase (a Waning Crescent Moon), not only is there little light, but what light there is continues to recede until it disappears. Not only is Luna reflecting scant luminescence, but during this phase it isn't really even our evening companion. Rising at pre-dawn, it follows us through the day rather than at night.

Without our sky-bound lunar beacon of light, we quest for another source of illumination. To discover it, we can turn within to the sanctum of our heart and mind. The route to accessing these reservoirs of wisdom is through quietude and reflection. We find ourselves with a greater receptivity, tapping into our intuition, attuned to what it is that moves, touches, and inspires us. Discovering the light within is a hallmark of the Balsamic Moon.

As we're at the end of the waning stage, we experience the continued encouragement to reduce rather than grow, release rather than acquire. As such, this isn't a time to begin new endeavors, to actively set about achieving goals. That moment will arrive soon when the next lunar cycle begins and the New Moon reappears overhead. For now, we relax, renew, and release, opening to the flow of what arises in this majestically liminal time.

In our fast-paced modern world, filled with the pressures of achievement, we often default to a constant need for action and a penchant for forward movement. During the days of the Balsamic Moon, we are called to do things a different way: to flow, to rest, and to allow. If ever we find this challenging, looking to the name of this period can serve as a powerful reminder of the essential benefits it embodies. The word *balsamic* comes from *balsam*, a sap or resin used for its medicinal properties. It is also referred to as *balm*, something known for its soothing and restorative qualities. Reflecting this, the Balsamic Moon can be quite a healing time. If we go with its flow, it can offer us a salve that inspires us with wisdom, infuses us with compassion, and replenishes us mind, body, and soul.

The Invitation: Renewal

As we reach the final stage of the lunar cycle, we shift our focus inward. It's a time of renewal, in which we become present to liminality, discover the power inherent in releasing things, and experience the beauty of being more receptive.

LIMINALITY

The Balsamic Moon is a very liminal period, one that seems filled with a sense of in-between, of being neither here nor there. We're not actively focusing on what we made manifest over the past three-plus weeks, nor are we consciously directing our attention to what will come next. And with that, there is only one place to be: in the rich space of the moment. To open to the beauty of this lunar phase, we can heed the sage counsel of spiritual teacher Ram Dass and "Be here now."

Liminality is a term coined by ethnographer Arnold van Gennep in his early twentieth century work, *Les Rites de Passage*, and later expanded upon in the 1960s by anthropologist Victor Turner. It refers to an essential period inherent in transformation, in which we have departed from a space we inhabited but have not arrived where we are headed. It is said to exist for both individuals and collectives, referring to either a time or space that is a passageway from one stage of development to the next.

Liminality derives from the Latin root *limen*, meaning *threshold*. A threshold is a piece of material at the bottom of a doorway that you step over to enter one room, thereby leaving another. It is also defined as a point in which an effect begins to be produced as well as a level above which something has veracity. We should embrace the liminality of the Balsamic Moon as a threshold, a period in which we are both walking away from something and walking toward another. Remembering this will give us faith, as well as additional clarity if things feel obscured, allowing us to more fully embrace the potential of this deeply alchemical time.

RELEASE

As the Balsamic Moon is the last phase of the lunar cycle, it is not a period to initiate anything new. It's a time for endings rather than beginnings. We release the need to be active and the urge to direct much of our energy outward. Instead, we let ourselves flow, instinctively knowing what wants to remain and what wants to slip away.

This sense of release is different than at the Last Quarter Moon (see page 82). There we diligently pruned; through conscious attention we saw what it was that we wanted to relinquish and did so. Now, we give over to quiet and silence. We revel in the power of the pause and the idea of taking a siesta. Awareness comes through witnessing what gets washed to the shore of our consciousness as well as what the tides of time want to take out to sea.

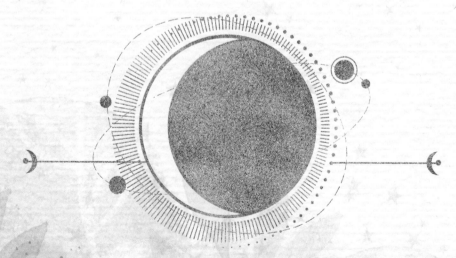

While it's not a moment to begin something new, we may discover that certain kernels of insight emerge—those that may presage upcoming passages. This makes sense when we consider that in the planting cycle this lunar phase is associated with the seed being released from the fruit and going back to the ground.

It's not just the endeavor we've been working on for the past three-plus weeks that we release during the Balsamic Moon. There are numerous other things that we may find ourselves called to surrender. These may be objects, but they may just as likely be ways of orienting. We may find that within this liminal space we are more apt to heed the call to renounce judgments, the need for control, and our desire to have things be exactly as we had previously envisioned. As we forfeit them, there arises a softness and compassion from which forgiveness can spring forth, further allowing us to release any frustrations or upsets that we've collected along our path.

BE RECEPTIVE

The Balsamic Moon is a time in which we embody the passive process of allowance. We are more apt to notice what arises when we make space and invite in stillness. We are open to receiving and find ourselves more attuned to being receptive. Our intuition is heightened, our imagination more unfettered, and our ability to feel a sense of interconnectivity magnified. It's a soulful time in which our connection to the numinous may feel more pronounced. It is also one in which we can open our arms and embrace the whispers of insights arising from our subconscious mind, which want to be seen and acknowledged.

We may find ourselves more capable of perceiving things that reside at the threshold: the subtle notes within a song, the meaning of a poem that has before eluded us, or what is inherent in our lover's glance . . . these are some of the things, often out of sight, that may be more in our line of vision at this time. It's not a time to push or to pull, but to be and to receive. In that peaceful space of receptivity, we perceive what emerges. We do so

Tarot Reflections: The High Priestess

The High Priestess tarot card invites us to retreat within. Instead of residing fully in our conscious mind, it invites us to traverse our subconscious. From this locale, we can discover greater wisdom. The card's emphasis on the power of stillness and contemplation is exquisitely aligned with the Balsamic Moon phase. The archetype of the High Priestess reminds us that we have all the answers within us, and that our intuition is a fount of stellar awareness. We just need to trust it, and to have faith that if we ask, we shall receive. To do so, carve out quiet time to go within. Like in this lunar phase, this tarot card reminds us that great knowledge can be accessed through reflection. The correlation between these two—the High Priestess and the Balsamic Moon (also known as the Waning Crescent Moon)—is also represented in the design of the card. In most decks, at the bottom of the image, you will find a crescent moon.

without preconceptions or judgements, as these often constrict our ability to open to the spectrum of possibility and see all that wants to be seen.

With allowance as our ally and a sense of openness a compass that directs us through these days, boundaries arise as a prominent theme during the Balsamic Moon. Steeped in liminality, we can cross through them more readily. As a time in which we have greater receptivity, we need to watch that we don't overstep boundaries that others have, nor allow them to do the same to us. Withdrawing into the sanctuary of our inner world—which this lunar phase inspires us to do—may be just what it takes to best navigate our boundaries, as well as to tap into something else that this lunar phase encourages: the expression of unconditional love.

STELLAR REFLECTION QUESTIONS

Here are some journaling prompts to work with during the Balsamic Moon. They can help you navigate through this time with more clarity, further connecting to the insights and awareness that this lunar phase offers.

What in my life wants to be released right now?

....

....

By inviting in more quiet, what awareness am I tuning into?

....

....

What thresholds do I feel I am crossing?

....

....

To whom can I offer forgiveness?

....

....

....

What are some of my favorite ways to relax?

....

....

....

How can I better take care of my mental and emotional well-being?

....

....

....

Self-Care Activities

We can sequence our self-care efforts during the month to align with the opportunities, challenges, and stress patterns that may inherently arise during each lunar phase. Here are several activities to practice during the Balsamic Moon.

TUNE INTO SILENCE

In this quiet and inward time, silence is just what we need to further connect to the voice of wisdom that lives within us. Ideas abound on how to do this without ferrying yourself away to a silent retreat (although that's an idea as well). Instead of listening to music while on a walk, opt for the sounds of the environment around you. During the day, put your phone on do-not-disturb mode for a while to avoid the pings of calls, texts, and other notifications that can interrupt your flow. Practice mindful eating, in which you eat in silence, focusing upon nothing else but the sensations you experience. And, of course, silent meditation is a great way to instill more serenity. Even if your mind seems noisy, taking the time to notice your thoughts will lead to more inner stillness.

HONOR THE DARK

Tap into the healing and relaxing properties of darkness during the Balsamic Moon. Dim the overhead lights or turn them off completely and illuminate your environment with candles. Doing so while you're taking a bath, listening to music, or enjoying a meal will allow you to sink more deeply into relaxation. Enjoy more dark foods, such as black beans, blueberries, dark chocolate, sea vegetables, and black rice, all of which feature an abundance of health-promoting phytonutrients. Mire yourself in mineral-rich mud or ventilated green clay; applying a mask to your body or face can improve circulation and aid in detoxification. Looking for a simple solution for cleaner water? Add a stick of Japanese charcoal to a water pitcher. If you're a crystal lover, spend time with dark gemstones such as onyx, obsidian, or shungite, placing them on your desk or altar during the Balsamic Moon. And, to feel more enveloped in darkness while you slumber, make sure to completely pull the blinds and/or don a sleep mask.

CONNECT TO YOUR DREAMS

The darkness we associate with our sleeping mind can actually be a reservoir of illumination if we turn to our dreams for awareness. During our oneiric journeys, we can tap into buried feelings, hidden motivations, and creative solutions, bringing them to light. While dreams can be a source of inspiration at any time, if you only want to focus on them once during the month, consider doing so at the Balsamic Moon. Place a journal and writing instrument by your bedside so that you can readily write down what you recall from your dreams. To further tune into what you've just experienced over the past almost-month, practice dream incubation. In this ritual, as you're about to drift off to sleep, intentionally pose a question to yourself about something that has been eluding you and about which you want more awareness. When you arise, reflect upon your dream to see if it contains the valuable answers you were seeking. Additionally, given that the Moon rises in the pre-dawn hours during this lunar phase, pay special attention to your early morning dreams as they may be more vivid and luminous.

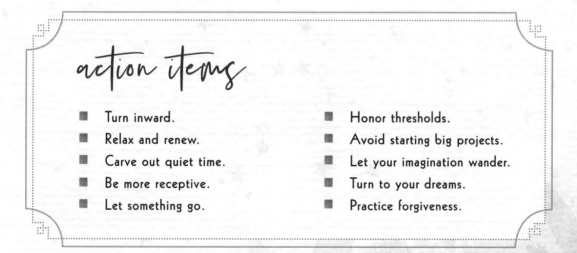

action items

- Turn inward.
- Relax and renew.
- Carve out quiet time.
- Be more receptive.
- Let something go.
- Honor thresholds.
- Avoid starting big projects.
- Let your imagination wander.
- Turn to your dreams.
- Practice forgiveness.

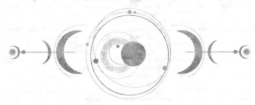

CHAPTER 10

MOON MAPPING JOURNAL GUIDES

You can use the following format as a guide to document what occurs for you during each of the eight lunar phases. First document the dates that each phase occurs. Then under *Stellar Reflections*, note the thoughts and feelings that arise, and in *Inspired Activities*, write down the actions you're taking and the aims you're pursuing. Dedicate the *Radical Realizations* section to any breakthroughs and discoveries that occur. You can then take the highlights you've captured and use them to fill in the Moon Mapping Mandala (page 104).

moon mapping journal

NEW MOON | INTENTION

Dates: _____

Stellar Reflections

_____

_____

_____

Inspired Activities

_____

_____

_____

Radical Realizations

_____

_____

_____

CRESCENT MOON | INITIATION

Dates: _____

Stellar Reflections

_____

_____

_____

Inspired Activities

_____

_____

_____

Radical Realizations

_____

_____

_____

FIRST QUARTER MOON | ACTION

Dates: _____

Stellar Reflections

_____

_____

_____

Inspired Activities

_____

_____

_____

Radical Realizations

_____

_____

_____

GIBBOUS MOON | REFINEMENT

Dates: _____

Stellar Reflections

_____
_____
_____

Inspired Activities

_____
_____
_____

Radical Realizations

_____
_____
_____

FULL MOON | ILLUMINATION

Dates: _____

Stellar Reflections

_____
_____
_____

Inspired Activities

_____
_____
_____

Radical Realizations

_____

_____

_____

DISSEMINATING MOON | SHARING

Dates: _____

Stellar Reflections

_____

_____

_____

Inspired Activities

_____

_____

_____

Radical Realizations

_____

_____

_____

LAST QUARTER MOON | MATURITY

Dates: _____

Stellar Reflections

_____

_____

_____

Inspired Activities

_____

_____

_____

Radical Realizations

_____

_____

_____

BALSAMIC MOON | RENEWAL

Dates: _____

Stellar Reflections

_____

_____

_____

Inspired Activities

_____

_____

_____

Radical Realizations

_____

_____

_____

Moon Mapping Mandala

The lunar cycle flows in a circular fashion, with each phase informed by the one that precedes it and seeding inspiration for the one that follows. Seeing the realizations you've had during each in the context of the others can give you a holistic view of your monthly journey. It can also lead to understanding connections that you hadn't previously perceived. This is the aim of the Moon Mapping Mandala.

On the following page, you will see the Moon Mapping Mandala diagram that you can use as a guide to create something similar in your personal and private journal, either in physical or electronic form. By each of the lunar phases, write in the dates for the current lunar cycle. Then, as you complete the different sections of the Moon Mapping Journal (page 98), transfer some of the highlights here, writing them by each of the corresponding circles. In the center, add your current New Moon Intention as well as your Moon Mapping Manifestation, which you created over the last four weeks. If you'd like to keep a record of your intentions and manifestations over the year, use the Intention and Manifestation Chronicle on page 106.

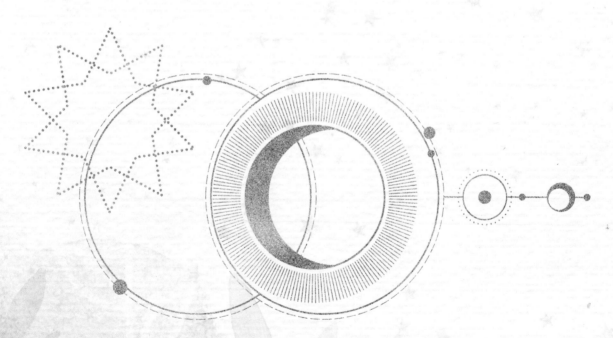

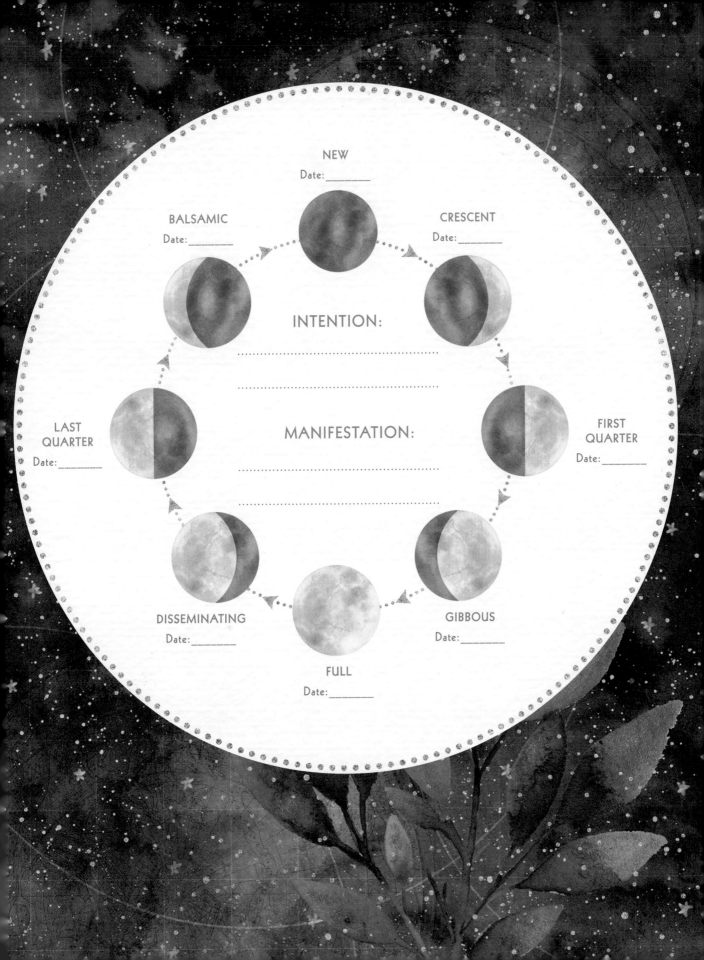

NEW

Date:_____

BALSAMIC

Date:_____

CRESCENT

Date:_____

INTENTION:

....

....

MANIFESTATION:

LAST
QUARTER

Date:_____

FIRST
QUARTER

Date:_____

....

....

DISSEMINATING

Date:_____

GIBBOUS

Date:_____

FULL

Date:_____

INTENTION AND MANIFESTATION CHRONICLE

Here's a simple way to track all your Moon Mapping Intentions
and Manifestations throughout the year.

New Moon Date: ....

Intention: ....

Manifestation: ....

New Moon Date: ....

Intention: ....

Manifestation: ....

New Moon Date: ....

Intention: ....

Manifestation: ....

New Moon Date: ....

Intention: ....

Manifestation: ....

New Moon Date: ....

Intention: ....

Manifestation: ....

New Moon Date: ....

Intention: ....

Manifestation: ....

New Moon Date: ....

Intention: ....

Manifestation: ....

New Moon Date: ....

Intention: ....

Manifestation: ....

New Moon Date: ....

Intention: ....

Manifestation: ....

New Moon Date: ....

Intention: ....

Manifestation: ....

New Moon Date: ....

Intention: ....

Manifestation: ....

New Moon Date: ....

Intention: ....

Manifestation: ....

New Moon Date: ....

Intention: ....

Manifestation: ....

the astrological moon

CHAPTER 11

AN INTRODUCTION TO THE ASTROLOGICAL MOON

Now that you've seen how tuning into the lunar phases can help you align with the times, let's explore another way that the Moon can connect you to stellar awareness: by looking at where it was when you were born. We call this our personal Moon or our natal Moon. It's also often referred to as the Moon in our chart. Regardless of its moniker, knowing more about it can be an essential element in creating a well-lived life.

You likely know your Sun sign, what you answer when someone asks, "What's your sign?" But did you know that, when it comes to gaining personalized insights through astrology, your Sun sign is only the beginning? Just as the Sun represents your vitality and what makes you shine, all the other planets are associated with distinct facets of who you are. By knowing them, you can more fully see the unique signature that you hold—what makes you *you*.

Which brings us back to the Moon.

Learning about your personal Moon can unlock a trove of treasures. It can help you further understand yourself, notably when it comes to your emotions and how being in tune with your feelings can help you more confidently navigate your life. The astrological Moon represents Mother, our perceptions of how we were mothered, and how we hold that role for others. Luna represents what we need and how we instinctively get our needs met. Through it we can understand who, what, and where has us feeling most at home

109

and that we truly belong. The Moon, as a container and reflector of the Sun's light, is also the celestial body that represents our body—that which embodies the solar spark of life—as well as our attitudes toward it. Therefore, knowing about your Moon can not only be a gateway to being more emotionally intelligent but can also help you know how to better take care of your health and well-being.

In addition to reflecting facets of your essential nature, your natal Moon can also help you pinpoint important times in your life. You can discover days each month and throughout the year when you can gain access to more knowledge about how to both clarify your needs and get them met. These Moon Moments can also help you to discern different periods of life when you can access a more fully embodied understanding of how your feelings can inspire and guide you.

In this part of the book, you'll explore all of this. Here you will find the following chapters:

- The Signs of the Moon:
  In these chapters, you'll discover key elements of each of the twelve Moon signs. You'll gain knowledge about:
  - Your Emotional Signature, including your essential needs, superpowers, and kryptonite

More Moon Factors

While your Moon sign and house will give you stellar insights, there are additional ways to learn more about yourself through this astrological factor, including the relationship that it makes with other planets and the Moon phase under which you were born. While these are beyond the scope of this book, you can find ways to further explore them in the Resources section on page 219.

- Your Stellar Self-Care, including nurturing strategies, stress spotlight, and health focus
- Your Sun + Moon sign pairing

- The Moon Through the Houses: When you look at your personal astrology chart, you see how your Moon falls in one of twelve houses, domains that represents different realms of life. In this chapter, you'll learn more about that astrological house so you can further know how to design your life so that it best serves you.

- Moon Moments: Here you'll discover how you can look to your Moon to gather insights into what different periods of your life hold when it comes to further embracing your lunar nature: your emotional capacity and ability to take care of yourself and others. You'll also see how to tap into the daily zeitgeist by knowing the zodiac sign that the Moon is in each day.

Through astrology apps, software programs, and online calculators, you can easily determine your Moon sign and house as well as Moon Moments. See page 219 to find resources that will enable you to do so.

What the Moon Represents

- What we find nourishing
- How we feed ourselves
- Our emotional nature
- How we feel about expressing our emotions
- Our perception of our mother
- Our style of mothering
- How we were nurtured as a child
- How we take care of ourselves and others
- Our home and what makes us feel at home
- Our body and how we take care of it
- Our inner self
- What has us feel safe and secure
- Our connection to the past
- Instinctive habits
- Cravings
- Subconscious mind
- A sense of belonging
- The place we return when we want to feel supported

CHAPTER 12

ARIES

SYMBOL

The Ram, an animal known for its strength, will, and competitive nature.

PLANETARY RULER

Mars, which represents desire, courage, self-initiation, and a call to action.

ELEMENT

Fire, characterized by the dynamic energy of inspiration, enthusiasm, and passion.

MODALITY

Cardinal, which prizes initiation, ambition, and being enterprising.

Your Emotional Signature

As the Moon symbolizes instinctive feelings, the sign in which it resides gives us more awareness about the nuances of our emotional nature. Knowing this can help us discern our essential needs, strengthen our superpowers, and be aware of our kryptonite (personal habits that can be challenging).

YOUR ESSENTIAL NEEDS

✳ *Being in Action*

You're endowed with a wellspring of energy and a desire to take action at every turn. Being in movement is not only natural to you but it's something that you need to feel fully alive. As such, regular exercise may really soothe your soul; not only does it have you feeling stronger, which is important to your inner warrior, but it also serves as a release valve for all the pent-up energy you carry. As your mind, often careening at a quick clip, loves to also be on the move, you have little patience for learning environments in which the pace is too slow and leisurely. Additionally, with your need for motion, it's important that you perceive that things in your life are progressing; after all, when you encounter stasis, you may feel that your inner flame has been dampened, which could lead to a sense that your spirit is, too.

✳ *Being a Pioneer*

As Aries is the initial sign of the zodiac, bursting on to the scene before others, leading the charge is routine for you. With your competitive nature, you're drawn to be the first one out of the gate. You dash forward quickly, excited for a new experience. You love the prospect of a new chapter, with the primary stages of any event being the ones for which you have the most interest and energy. You're a pathfinder, who has the instinct and courage to proceed down avenues that others may not have ever considered, let alone heard of. Whether you're a pioneer in your career field, the first in your family to go to grad school, or the one known to get up at the crack of dawn to secure those sought-after concert tickets, as an Aries Moon, it feels good to be ahead of the pack.

✳ *Championing Causes*

Really tuning into what you desire—what ignites you mind, body, and soul—is essential to someone with an Aries Moon. It feeds your fire and helps you discover outlets toward which to direct the excitement and enthusiasm you have for life. And when you combine your passions with your feisty warrior spirit, you have an arsenal that will help you triumph in the pursuit of any cause you want to champion. Applying your sparring nature to *fight for* something that deeply ignites you may also tender another benefit: your being less likely to manifest situations that require you to *fight against* something or someone. Not only will you discover numerous triumphs through being an active champion, but your life may be filled with fewer battles and more peace.

YOUR SUPERPOWERS

✳ *Courage*

When facing a new opportunity, you don't inundate yourself with "what ifs" and "should I's." Rather, you greet situations—whether they be inspiring or challenging—with a daring spirit unencumbered by the fears held by many. Instead of worrying about what could happen four steps down the line, your reverence for the here and now has you tuned into what's right in front of you. This enables you to jump squarely into the middle of the action with the heroism for which you are known.

✳ *Spark*

You're burnished with excitement when you encounter novel experiences and meet new people. This gives you a zest for life that really rubs off on others. Your enthusiasm can often be like fairy dust that makes others smile and galvanizes them into action. It can also help you enlist people to see projects through to their end. This way you can turn your attention to starting something new, the stage of creation where you feel the most energized.

✳ *Passion*

Your desires run deep and fuel your movements. They carry you quickly into the center of anything that ignites and attracts you, emboldening your ability to take risks that others may not. Whatever fans your fire motivates you into action, whether it be that special someone or that special idea. Your passion is part of your raison d'être. Even if others find your fervent nature sometimes too hot to handle, never quash the gift that is your ardor-filled spirit.

YOUR KRYPTONITE

✳ *Restlessness*

With your love of being on the move, sometimes it's hard for you to slow down. Doing so may leave you fidgety, cause your nerves to become jittery, and prompt a sense of disquietude to prevail. Your desire for motion also extends to your mind, which can whirl with thoughts and a frayed attention span when you're stressed. To counter being wound up, weave winding-down strategies—such as deep breathing, a walk outside, and/or a short meditation practice—into your daily routine.

✳ *Boredom*

You love beginnings and all the promise and potential they hold. And while this has you galvanized in the kickoff phase of any project, it often has your interest plummeting soon after. This can inspire impatience and lead to ennui, a boredom that can have you prematurely abandon what you're involved in so that you can move on to the next thing. Structuring your objectives so that they contain distinct mini-goals that you can readily achieve may help you keep your long-term attention piqued.

✳ *Temper*

With your passionate nature and fighting spirit, if you don't get what you want as rapidly as you'd like, your temper may flare. And while your anger often resolves as quickly as it appears, your short-fused outbursts may cause quite the rattle; this may not only upset others but stir your stress levels. Plus, it can lead you into battles that you later regret. Try to tone down your temper when you know it's at odds with getting your needs met.

Your Stellar Self-Care

As the Moon corresponds to our physical body as well as what we find nourishing, the sign of its placement gives us insights into how to best take care of ourselves. Here you'll find nurturing strategies, tips to overcome what causes you stress, and a health focus to pay attention to.

NURTURING STRATEGIES

✳ *Big Benefits for Little Time*

Let's face it: you prefer things that take less time than more, activities that don't require your singular attention for that long. You're much more interested in having a multitude of short experiences rather than a few longer ones. The good news is that you can honor your need to move at a quick clip without having to skimp on your self-care. Chair massages and express manicures are two examples of services that pack a wellness punch in a small bite of time. Circuit training may also be interesting to you as it concentrates numerous activities into one workout. And, if meditating for twenty minutes at a stretch feels like a stretch, break it up into several five-minute mini-mindfulness sessions.

✳ *Being a Health Champion*

A warrior at heart, you will fight for anything to which you set your mind. So, when you turn your attention to your well-being, you may find that nothing can stand in your way of pursuing feeling your very best. And even if you go through periods of not focusing on your fitness, the minute the urge to get in shape catches your attention, trust that you'll hop right back in the driver's seat and proceed quickly toward your health goals. You can use your strong will and determination to not only push you to the front lines of any health battle, but also to the front of any line to ensure you can quickly access a service that you feel will be beneficial.

✳ *Inspiring Fire*

As a fire sign, Aries likes it hot. With your Moon located here, channel your natural affinity for high temperatures, choosing nurturing wellness activities that incorporate the healing power of heat. For example, a hot stone massage can be really relaxing, melting away muscular tension and stress. Taking a sauna or steam bath can envelop you with warmth while also helping you to sweat out impurities. Start your day in a fiery way by drinking warm water peppered with lemon juice, maple syrup, and a dash of cayenne, which will get your mind and body moving in no time. Additionally, ask your acupuncturist about moxibustion, a treatment that uses heated mugwort to stimulate blood circulation and open up energy channels.

STRESS SPOTLIGHT

✳ *Impatience*

You have a fast pace and often move in haste, getting easily frustrated when you're ready to do something and the rest of the world isn't. If people take too long or things are delayed, you may find yourself bristling with impatience and the short fuse that often accompanies it. Not only may this amplify your stress levels, it can also cause you to make rash decisions that moments later you really regret. When you find your patience wearing thin and want to catch yourself before irascibility sets in, consider this strategy: take ten deep breaths, scan your body for tension, and then focus on relaxing any tight muscles. Repeating affirmations such as "I have all the time in the world" can also be really helpful. If you're looking for a flower essence to help you quell impatience and the irritation that often accompanies it, try Impatiens.

HEALTH FOCUS

✳ *Head*

As Aries governs the head, those with their Moon in this sign may find this to be a spot in which their tension often takes residence. A headache may be one of the first signals that something is out of balance and that your stress levels are elevated. And, as much as you may want to charge right through the discomfort and keep moving ahead, a headache is something that can actually stop the nonstop Aries Moon right in its tracks.

Luckily, there are some natural strategies that can help you deal with—and perhaps avoid—a throbbing noggin. Do an inventory of what you eat to notice if any particular foods trigger headaches, avoiding them for two weeks to see if your symptoms subside. Weave relaxation practices into your day: walking meditation may be a good choice since it allows you to find center while still honoring your active self. Keep yourself hydrated by drinking about eight glasses of water daily. And for those with migraines, look to eliminate food triggers such as aged cheese, sour cream, red wine, and chocolate. For some people, low magnesium levels are a headache trigger. Try adding leafy greens, nuts, and seeds to your diet to amplify your intake of this precious nutrient.

Your Sun + Your Moon

Now that you know more about your Moon sign, it's interesting to think about it in relationship with your Sun sign. As these two luminaries are at the foundation of our essential sense of self, looking at your Sun and Moon as a pair can give you additional insights to further understand yourself. Below you will find the twelve pairings associated with the Aries Moon.

☀ + ☾		PROFILE
ARIES	**ARIES**	As a double Aries, you love to be on the move. It's important for you to be in action, taking the helm to pursue what you desire. The playing field is where you love to be; waiting on the sidelines is not your jam. Just watch that impatience doesn't get the best of you.
TAURUS	**ARIES**	At times you move leisurely while at others you can't proceed fast enough; honoring both is key to your happiness. With an Aries Moon, you can champion the practical approaches that your Taurus Sun cherishes. Spending time outdoors, notably during seasonal shifts when change is afoot, can bring you joy.
GEMINI	**ARIES**	Keeping things fresh and interesting is really important to you. You like going to battle for your ideas and are quite good at it. With a curious Gemini Sun and pioneering Aries Moon, you're interested in having conversations that allow you to explore new territories.
CANCER	**ARIES**	Given your affinity for the fresh and new, changing up your home's décor now and again may make it feel even more nurturing. With a protective Cancer Sun and an assertive Aries Moon, if your loved ones or prized possessions are threatened, you will passionately jump into the fray to defend them.
LEO	**ARIES**	You've got boldness and gumption. You exhibit courage in many ways, including having a strong capacity to navigate life with an open heart. With your Sun in generous Leo and your Moon in passionate Aries, your deep desires guide your movements and help you chart your course.

PROFILE

VIRGO	ARIES	Sometimes you're precise and at other times you like to wing it. And while having things be organized is important, at times your patience can wear thin waiting for that to happen. Your Virgo Sun is inclined to help others live a better life, and your Aries Moon gives you the spunk to fight for those aims.
LIBRA	ARIES	Balancing your Libra Sun's affinity for fairness with your Aries Moon moxie, you can be a warrior for peace and justice. You have a strong desire to forge alliances. However, sometimes it can be frustrating when it requires too much work, or you feel that your own needs are stifled in a partnership.
SCORPIO	ARIES	You're quite fierce and passionate, inspired to fight for what you truly want. You're anything but timid when it comes to diving headfirst into emotionally stirring experiences. Balancing your Scorpio Sun's intensity with your Aries Moon's need to quickly change focus is key to feeling more at peace.
SAGITTARIUS	ARIES	With an exploratory nature, you're always ready for the next adventure and love having a queue of them to look forward to. With your enthusiastic Sagittarius Sun and excitement-loving Aries Moon, you've got a thirst for life and the cornucopia of experiences that it offers.
CAPRICORN	ARIES	Having a hardworking Capricorn Sun and a pioneering Aries Moon, you can be quite the entrepreneur. You prefer to work on the initial stages of a project and then pass it off to others to execute. This way you can move on to the thrill of beginning another venture.
AQUARIUS	ARIES	With an Aquarius Sun, you're cerebral and laid back, and yet with your Aries Moon, you're also fiery and love to be in the middle of the action. Being able to have distance allows you to get a clear picture of a situation. Once you do, you then stride in with full force to win the prize in which you are interested.
PISCES	ARIES	You're caring and compassionate as well as fierce and passionate. When you're feeling aligned, you can be an empathetic warrior who fights for those who need a champion. With a Pisces Sun, you love to go with the flow, and yet your feisty Aries Moon often takes no prisoners.

CHAPTER 13

TAURUS

SYMBOL

The Bull, an animal known for its strength, stamina, and confidence.

ELEMENT

Earth, characterized by the grounded energy of creativity, resilience, and practicality.

PLANETARY RULER

Venus, which represents love, beauty, and the force of attraction.

MODALITY

Fixed, which prizes reliability, predictability, and stamina.

Your Emotional Signature

As the Moon symbolizes instinctive feelings, the sign in which it resides gives us more awareness about the nuances of our emotional nature. Knowing this can help us discern our essential needs, strengthen our superpowers, and be aware of our kryptonite (personal habits that can be challenging).

YOUR ESSENTIAL NEEDS

✳ *Finding a Rhythm*

You groove when you feel you're in a groove. After all, connecting to a sense of consistency is inherently important to those with Taurus Moons; having regularity can provide you with satisfaction on the regular. There's something about the reliability of knowing what's next that is very soothing to you. That's likely part of the reason that change is often so challenging: it disturbs the flow of your steady tempo, plus being in flux can feel really ungrounding. Tune in to your personal rhythms to understand how to sequence your routines so that they can have you feeling your very best. Consider, for example, your sleep patterns: on the days that you feel the most energized and full of concentration, how much sleep did you get and at what time did you get into bed? Once you identify this, arrange your schedule so that you can follow this vitality-supporting regimen.

✳ *Living Sensually*

Taurus is the sign associated with the five senses, and those with their Moon placed here gain great comfort—let alone gratification—by experiencing life through these modes of perception. Whether it's the smell of fresh-cut grass, the radiant colors cast by a sunset, or the flavorful bounty of a fresh peach, for you, simple pleasures are never simple. You're sensitive somatically, and gentle touch—such as the way it feels when your lover strokes your arm or when a breeze sweeps across your face—can bring you delight. You've also got a keen acuity for sound and a love of music, which you find comforting and inspiring. When you're stressed, you likely indulge yourself even more than usual: this can be very nurturing if it's something like taking a leisurely bubble bath, but less so if it manifests in an extended rendezvous with a pint of ice cream.

✳ *Connecting with Nature*

As the first earth sign of the zodiac, Taurus instills a reverence for the environment. You prefer the natural to the synthetic, whether in fabrics, fragrances, or food. Speaking of the latter, it is something from which you derive great pleasure; you likely spend a good portion of energy, and perhaps even money, procuring and preparing it. Another way that you connect with nature is through tactile activities in which you create things: whether it's cooking, sculpting, or jewelry making, you enjoy pursuits that employ practical approaches and yield tangible outcomes. Gardening is another activity that can be nourishing. Whether you tend to numerous plants or grow a few herbs on your windowsill, it allows you to connect to the land and gain satisfaction by growing your own food. And, of course, being in nature—whether it's going for hikes, spending time in parks, or floating down a river—is quite soothing for your soul.

YOUR SUPERPOWERS

✳ *Practicality*

You have a propensity to look at things head on. Rather than getting side swiped by the what-ifs, you see the realities of what's in your sightline. When it comes to bringing plans to life, you have an uncanny finesse for knowing what's feasible and mustering the resources to manifest it using a no-nonsense approach. You're a master of the mundane: whether it's making restaurant reservations, researching insurance plans, or locating your favorite foods when traveling, you do it like a practicality pro.

✳ *Serenity*

Tranquility is the essence of your nature, and one of the reasons that people are so drawn to you. You're grounded and love to connect to the rhythms of the natural world, which you find pacifying. As you like to move at a slow and steady pace, your even-keeled spirit is a balm for others, notably when the world seems chaotic. You strive for peace and aim for calm, and with your strong desire to avoid sudden change, you have a serenity that is quite attractive.

✳ *Consistency*

Your reliability reigns supreme. Through thick and thin, you appear consistent. After all, moving slowly and steadily—whether physically or emotionally—feels quite nurturing to you. Your dependability informs your tempo and how people perceive you: as someone unwavering and in whose presence others trust they will feel more grounded and secure.

Given that your what-you-see-is-what-you-get character is steadily reassuring, people find themselves prone to rely upon you.

YOUR KRYPTONITE

✳ *Fear of Change*

Switching things up is hard for Taurus Moons. Your dislike of flux and your need to always know what comes next may have you anxious any time change looms on the horizon. Not only does this instill worry and disquietude, it could also have you arrange your life with such constancy that you miss out on exciting adventures. When it's time to change it up, doing so at a slow yet steady pace may help you make shifts with less stress.

✳ *Love of Lounging*

Feeling settled is much easier than exerting yourself too much, which can feel rattling to your gentle, slow-moving constitution. Combine that with your resistance to change and your love of luxuriating in your creature comforts, and sometimes you may find yourself on the slippery slope to laziness. While relaxing can have its boons, be careful that lassitude doesn't get in your way of giving shape and form to the goals that are important to you.

✳ *Stubbornness*

Another realm in which the motivation to move isn't necessarily second nature is your fixed nature. The comfort you feel from the known sometimes makes it hard for you to release the positions and perspectives you hold. Being stubborn definitely has its downsides: a headstrong orientation can ruffle feathers, while being overly set in your opinions may limit you from having enjoyable experiences. When you find yourself really digging in, question whether it's truly serving your highest good.

Your Stellar Self-Care

As the Moon corresponds to our physical body as well as what we find nourishing, the sign of its placement gives us insights into how to best take care of ourselves. Here you'll find nurturing strategies, tips to overcome what causes you stress, and a health focus to pay attention to.

NURTURING STRATEGIES

✳ *Going at a Slow Pace*

You love to move at a leisurely pace, preferring an unhurried tempo to a rapid stride. Finding exercise routines that don't push you to move fast can motivate you to keep moving. For example, long walks provide great benefits and may be easier to commit to than higher intensity workouts. There's also yin yoga, in which you hold poses for several minutes; it not only yields flexibility but enhances joint mobility and inspires calm. Weaving slowness into your fitness regimen can also benefit you another way: not rushing into your workouts—by building in time to wind up and wind down—can help you avoid sprains and strains that could otherwise arise if you proceed at a more hurried pace.

✳ *The Power of Touch*

You're highly connected to your body. You garner great pleasure through your senses, including the experience of being touched. Regular massages may not only help work out tension—including in your neck, a part of the body ruled by Taurus—but offer a tactile trajectory to enjoyment. Also consider treatments such as acupressure, body scrubs, and facials, all of which emphasize the power of touch. Additionally, don't be shy about your need for physical connection with those you love. Whether it's cuddling with your partner, holding hands with your child, or hugging your friends, physical affection can be quite nurturing and healing for you.

✳ *Tuning In*

While Taurus rules all five senses, given that it's the sign that governs the ears, it's especially aligned with hearing. As such, sound therapy may be a restorative practice of which you may want to take note. Some massage therapists work with tuning forks, special wands calibrated for different vibrations, thought to inspire energetic attunement. You could also listen to binaural beats, music that's composed so that each ear hears a different frequency tone. Many claim that this auditory experience leads to reduced stress, greater mental concentration, and better sleep. Remember, though, it's not just the presence of sound—but also its absence—that can be relaxing to those with Taurus Moons. For example, using earplugs or a noise machine at night may help you sleep better.

STRESS SPOTLIGHT

✳ *Uncertainty*

You often associate uncertainty with adversity, for fear that potential change will disrupt your steady flow, essential for your sense of security. It's part of what drives you to plan, believing that it will give you a greater ability to respond to any unknown that's just around the corner. Yet, even with all the practical steps you undertake, it sometimes doesn't stave off the disquietude that comes from your aversion to being in flux. It's important to remember that the nature of nature is change, and to be confident that you have the resources necessary to navigate periods of transition. Meditation can be a helpful practice to keep you present and centered through the natural shifts that life brings. If you want additional support in facing the unknown, and more fortitude to navigate unchartered territories, consider Aspen flower essence.

HEALTH FOCUS

✳ *Throat*

The throat is one of the parts of the body under the domain of Taurus. And with that, it's a spot to give extra TLC since it can be an area where your stress accumulates. Sore throats can be painful and frustrating. And dysphonia, commonly known as hoarseness—which may be caused by a cold, sinus infection, gastroesophageal reflux (GERD), aging, or just using your voice too much—can make it challenging to communicate.

Staying hydrated by consuming adequate amounts of water is one powerful and simple pillar of throat care. And if your throat hurts, try gargling with salt water. Enjoying tea made with a drop of raw honey and herbs such as slippery elm and marshmallow may also be helpful, as can a throat spray made from bee propolis and/or throat-soothing herbs such as sage and mullein. It's also important to exercise your voice: regularly communicate your needs and also flex your vocal muscles by belting out tunes on occasion (even if only in the privacy of your shower or car). Ever find that your throat feels tight or that it's challenging to swallow at times? If so, speak with your healthcare practitioner to see whether the cause may be too many acidic foods causing laryngopharyngeal reflux (also known as silent reflux).

Your Sun + Your Moon

Now that you know more about your Moon sign, it's interesting to think about it in relationship with your Sun sign. As these two luminaries are at the foundation of our essential sense of self, looking at your Sun and Moon as a pair can give you additional insights to further understand yourself. Below you will find the twelve pairings associated with the Taurus Moon.

☀ + ☽		PROFILE
ARIES	**TAURUS**	You're that unique blend of pioneering and practical. With your Aries Sun, you like to champion causes, and with your Taurus Moon, these may include subjects relating to the natural world. You've got a tricky relationship with patience: at times it easily wears thin, while at other times you're quite happy if things proceed leisurely.
TAURUS	**TAURUS**	As a double Taurus, you really love your creature comforts. Being surrounded by luxurious objects that delight your senses is quite inspiring. You handle practical matters with finesse. As you place a high prize on security, making money and managing your finances is important to you.
GEMINI	**TAURUS**	As a Gemini Sun, you want to educate others; given that you have a Taurus Moon, the subject matters in which you're interested may include nature, art, and practical matters. Sometimes you like to move quickly, and other times slowly; finding opportunities that allow you to do both is elemental to your happiness.
CANCER	**TAURUS**	You love learning about food, preparing it, and enjoying it with others; after all, your Cancer Sun loves feeling nourished while your Taurus Moon has a sybaritic side. Home is really important, and you want yours to be beautiful, as it's that special spot where you nest and build memories with those closest to you.
LEO	**TAURUS**	As a Leo Sun, you've got a creative bent, and with your Taurus Moon, you turn to the natural world as your muse. Not only do you love fun, but you also have quite a practical side. You've got a determined personality and maybe even a bit of a stubborn streak as well.

☀ + ☾

VIRGO · **TAURUS**

You're an artisan who really prizes beauty, which for you means that aesthetics are partially rooted in something's functionality. Being with nature is very satisfying. With your Virgo Sun, you can be a very hard worker, notably if you align your aims with the practical matters that your Taurus Moon prizes.

LIBRA · **TAURUS**

You're a lover of luxury. You have a strong affinity for things infused with beauty and that yield pleasure and delight. While with a Libra Sun, it may take you some time to make decisions, once you do, your Taurus Moon inspires you to commit and stay the course.

SCORPIO · **TAURUS**

You're guided by both emotionality and practicality, able to survey things on the surface and also dive below to find hidden treasures. With your tenacious Scorpio Sun and your consistent Taurus Moon, when you find something that deeply nourishes you, you hold on to it for a while.

SAGITTARIUS · **TAURUS**

You're a visionary who is nurtured by channeling your inspiration into practical ideas. You love traveling as it connects you to food, art, and landscapes that delight your senses. It's important to find a balance between your Sagittarius Sun's desire for action and your Taurus Moon's need for leisure.

CAPRICORN · **TAURUS**

For you, the tangible is where it's at. You love connecting to nature and building structures that have practical payoffs. With your responsible Capricorn Sun and your serene Taurus Moon, you're steady and even-keeled, qualities that can help you to accomplish your goals.

AQUARIUS · **TAURUS**

You're quite determined. When you set your mind to something, you like to see it through. You're both interested in larger world issues, thanks to your Aquarius Sun, and practical matters, thanks to your Taurus Moon. You've got the patience to bring about innovative solutions.

PISCES · **TAURUS**

You long to have your life filled with more beauty and grace. You take your Piscean ideals and make them manifest through the physical objects and intentional rituals your Taurus Moon adores. You're at once soulful while also grounded, a romantic dreamer who strives to feel connected to bodily pleasures.

CHAPTER 14

GEMINI

SYMBOL

The Twins, a pair that shares commonality while also expressing unique individuality.

PLANETARY RULER

Mercury, which represents the mind, communication, and language.

ELEMENT

Air, characterized by the agile energy of observation, logic, and sociability.

MODALITY

Mutable, which prizes flexibility, adaptability, and movement.

Your Emotional Signature

As the Moon symbolizes instinctive feelings, the sign in which it resides gives us more awareness about the nuances of our emotional nature. Knowing this can help us discern our essential needs, strengthen our superpowers, and be aware of our kryptonite (personal habits that can be challenging).

YOUR ESSENTIAL NEEDS

✳ *Being Mentally Stimulated*

You instinctively follow your sharp curiosity and allow your need-to-know to be your guide in gathering more knowledge. You're an equal-opportunity collector of insights: you're just as happy to get the lowdown on a trivial fact as you are on a broader subject. As a lover of variety, you're drawn to accessing multiple sources of information at a time. It's not uncommon for you to have numerous tabs on your browser open at once or a stack of partially read books on your nightstand. You love to keep your mind active and also actively expand it—something that all the time you spend reading, thinking, wordsmithing, and conversing brings you in spades. Your desire to be intellectually aroused may also forge the basis of your sexual attraction; even if someone is really good-looking, your passion for them may quickly wane if you don't find them mentally captivating.

✳ *Experiencing Variety*

The symbol for Gemini being the Twins is quite telling, reflecting your need for multiplicity rather than singularity. You have an aversion to being limited to solo options—it's a straight shot to boredom, the bane of your existence. Figuratively speaking, while some may prefer chocolate ice cream and others vanilla, you love both; sometimes you alternate your flavor choice, while at other times you opt for the swirl, which allows you to have the best of both worlds. If you are faced with situations in which you're unable to choose from an array of possibilities, it can leave you feeling like your freedom is curtailed. Your need for alternatives also extends to your perspectives and viewpoints. You see and appreciate both sides of every proverbial coin. And while doing so leads to holistic understanding, it can sometimes cause stress when it leaves you seeming fickle, unable to easily select a course of action.

✳ *Having Freedom of Movement*

Those with Gemini Moons are like butterflies, with a need to flit here and there, seeking the pollen of information from various sources. While this may sometimes manifest as restlessness, it actually stems from an underlying need to access the multitude of inputs you know to be necessary for holistic understanding. When traveling, you like to roam. You set out with curiosity as your trusted compass, meandering through neighborhoods, picking up fascinating facts about the local culture that you wouldn't have accessed had you followed a prescribed path. This need to feel unencumbered extends to your mind as well. With an ability to switch your attention at a moment's notice, you are able to work on several projects at once. What's more: having a collection of tasks to focus upon is not only interesting but also more efficient, as it allows you to readily take breakthroughs you have in one undertaking and immediately adapt them to another.

YOUR SUPERPOWERS

✳ *Amicability*

Your friendliness is magnetic. Between your youthful spirit, ability to converse with almost anyone, and congenial nature, others are drawn to you. Your affability is attractive, and people feel more spirited and energized in your presence, which often brings out their joy and generosity. Charm and friendliness are your calling cards. Not only are they the qualities people remember you for, they are also keys to your personal and professional success.

✳ *Flexibility*

You have an innate ability to be adaptive that allows you to pivot more readily than most, a talent that offers you numerous benefits. It keeps you open to new experiences through which you can learn. Plus, instead of being attached to a fixed path, your ability to be limber allows you to acclimate quite readily to new situations, sidestepping stress others may encounter. Your talent for staying bouncy can result in less tension and worry when change is afoot.

✳ *Communication Skills*

You're a source of information for people, a media outlet of your own making. As a quick-witted messenger who has a way with words, people come to you to learn from the fount of facts that you've collected throughout your life. Your affinity for communication gives you great skills to design communiqués to get your points across. You're also able to use your talents to be of service to those whose natural proclivity for language is not as stellar as yours.

YOUR KRYPTONITE

✳ *Overthinking*

Your bright mind is often your go-to for navigating the world. And while this can help you figure things out, it sometimes has you taking an overly rational route to life, one that prizes the logical at the expense of the emotional. Remember that along with your desire to scope out a gamut of perspectives, your feelings can also serve as a well of wisdom. Have your mindset be informed not only from your mind but also from your heart.

✳ *Distractibility*

You are interested in such a wide array of subjects that focusing on any one at a given time can sometimes be challenging. For example, you may find yourself researching a subject only to come across an ancillary fact that powerfully grabs your interest, sending you down a rabbit hole that's located far away from your original destination. Practicing mindfulness can keep you aware of when your mercurial mind wanders in a such a way that it diverts your attention.

✳ *Fickleness*

You change your mind often. It's not necessarily that you have commitment issues as much as that you can see the merits of multiple options. Unfortunately, this can sometimes lead to your seeming overly capricious, or leave you spinning your wheels when it comes to even the simplest of decisions. A strategy for when you find it challenging to make a choice: remember that another one in which you can choose differently is likely right around the corner.

Your Stellar Self-Care

As the Moon corresponds to our physical body as well as what we find nourishing, the sign of its placement gives us insights into how to best take care of ourselves. Here you'll find nurturing strategies, tips to overcome what causes you stress, and a health focus to pay attention to.

NURTURING STRATEGIES

* *Activities That Engage Your Mind*

As a person who spends a lot of time in thought, ensuring your mind is engrossed is an inherently important way to nourish yourself. Plus, it can be quite beneficial for your health; it's been found that challenging your brain to learn a new skill—for example, a foreign language, musical instrument, or dance style—can enhance your memory and keep your mind sharp as you age. Similarly, activities that involve learning or the sharing of ideas—whether journal writing, poetry reading, or talk therapy—may be attractive for those with a communicative Gemini Moon. And if you're looking for extra motivation to go on a long walk, consider chatting with a friend or listening to an audiobook while doing so.

* *Leaving Space for Spontaneity*

At times, you may find it challenging to stick to a fitness routine since you perceive it boring to do the same thing over again. Plus, like in everything you do, you savor variety and like to have the freedom to choose from a cornucopia of options. Here's a simple workout work-around to try if you're looking for a fitness regimen with flexibility. First, block out spots on your weekly schedule for exercise. Then, when it's time to work out, see what type of movement you're in the mood for. Perhaps it's a Pilates class on a streaming service, a mini-workshop at the local yoga studio, or some simple stretches done on your own. Engage in whatever you have an affinity for in the moment.

* *Being a Researcher*

Make elevating your well-being a puzzle you want to solve. Doing so will engage your inquisitive mind and give you another subject to research—one of your favorite activities. When looking for a new diet regimen, exercise routine, or relaxation practice, scour books, websites, and social media platforms to learn about what's hot and what's not. Additionally, broadcast your inquiry to your friends, family, and colleagues. They may not only be great sources of practical intelligence, but of conversations in which you can learn new things—a nourishing activity for you. Once you sift through your findings, consider taking on the mantle of messenger, a role that you love: write out all the resources you've discovered and share them with others.

STRESS SPOTLIGHT

✴ *Endless Thoughts*

You are nourished when you are learning, whether when seeking new facts and figures, contemplating insights, or solving problems. While your hunger for intellectual stimulation gives you a bright and active mind, it may also lead to an endless eddy of thoughts that could leave you nervous and stressed. Help quell agitation by grounding into your body: any time you find yourself spiraling, go for a walk, do some stretching, or even calm a jumpy mind by doing some jumping jacks. As Gemini rules the respiratory system, remember that focusing on your breath is an important part of self-care. Whether it's a daily breath-meditation session or doing deep diaphragmatic breathing throughout the day, you'll find yourself inhaling more peace and quietude. And, if you're looking for a flower essence to help you slow down the mental merry-go-round that you may experience, consider White Chestnut.

HEALTH FOCUS

✴ *Shoulders, Arms, and Hands*

Gemini, the Twins, has a connection to things that come in pairs. Therefore, it's no surprise that it's the sign that governs the shoulders, arms, and hands. Unfortunately, these are the most common sites for repetitive strain injury, which can arise from routine motion and bad posture. A common cause of this? Spending too much time on your computer, tablet, or phone—something you're likely doing often given your curious mind and affinity for knowledge.

If you find yourself with excess tension in your shoulders, nothing beats a regular massage to work out those kinks. A DIY approach for breaking up tension is a tennis ball massage, a series of exercises in which you place a small ball between you and a wall or the floor, and moving gently, work out myofascial tension. In addition, make sure your chair and desk are positioned so that you are ergonomically supported. Take breaks during long stints in front of your computer: get up and go on a short walk, or even do a few plank exercises, which will help strengthen your shoulders, arms, wrists, and core. Arnica ointment, CBD salves, and contrast hydrotherapy (where you alternate hot and cold compresses) can also be helpful to melt upper body tension.

Your Sun + Your Moon

Now that you know more about your Moon sign, it's interesting to think about it in relationship with your Sun sign. As these two luminaries are at the foundation of our essential sense of self, looking at your Sun and Moon as a pair can give you additional insights to further understand yourself. Below you will find the twelve pairings associated with the Gemini Moon.

☀ + ☾		PROFILE
ARIES	**GEMINI**	A Gemini Moon, with its need-to-know nature, augments an Aries Sun's interest in charting new paths. Your curiosity is a powerful tool in your arsenal for your pioneering endeavors. You've got a restless spirit that's always looking for fresh starts. Movement—both physical and mental—inspires you.
TAURUS	**GEMINI**	As a Taurus Sun, you are not keen on quick change. Conversely, with a Gemini Moon, you are nurtured when you exhibit your ability to adapt quickly. Your research skills come in handy when dealing with practical matters. Be open to the different paces that nurture you—fast at times, leisurely at others.
GEMINI	**GEMINI**	Being a double Gemini, you've got a quicksilver character, able to acclimate more readily than most to whatever arises in the moment. You possess a strong intellectual bent and like to understand things. And while keeping your mind engaged is motivating, be careful not to do so at the expense of taking care of your body.
CANCER	**GEMINI**	As a Cancer Sun, your feelings often hold sway. Although, instead of just riding with the tides of your emotions, your Gemini Moon finds them fascinating and feels drawn to analyze them from all directions. While understanding your feelings is important, just watch for a propensity to overintellectualize them.
LEO	**GEMINI**	Having a Gemini Moon gives a Leo Sun an extra dose of youthfulness and friendliness. You have the potential to be a very creative communicator who puts their unique stamp on the messages they share. You like to have fun and continually seek ways to express your love and generosity.

PROFILE

VIRGO	GEMINI	With your ability to marry your organizational abilities and your love of figuring out puzzles, your problem-solving skills are quite amazing. It's important to balance a push-pull between your Virgo Sun's desire to have things be neat and tidy and your Gemini Moon's need to have several plates in the air at any time.
LIBRA	GEMINI	You're quite a social creature, one who loves being in the company of others from whom you can learn. With your Gemini Moon's inquisitive nature, you're interested in understanding what makes people tick, a quality that can further forge the dynamic partnerships that your Libra Sun so cherishes.
SCORPIO	GEMINI	As a Scorpio Sun, you like to dig into matters of all kinds and figure out the mysteries of life. Add to that your Gemini Moon's natural affinity for information-gathering and you're a researcher par excellence. Finding ways to integrate your hyper-focused nature and your mercurial side will help keep you balanced.
SAGITTARIUS	GEMINI	As a Sagittarius, you're an explorer at heart. And with a Gemini Moon, you're interested in quests that expand your mind. You not only love to learn but also to share your experiences with others. You have an uncanny way to gather facts that can support the larger concepts in which you are interested.
CAPRICORN	GEMINI	As a Capricorn Sun, you're a doer, while with a Gemini Moon you're also a thinker. It's important to give space to both approaches to life, while also seeing how they can complement each other. Respect your need for structure and tradition while also finding ways to honor your desire for variety and change.
AQUARIUS	GEMINI	With both your Sun and Moon in air signs, there's a simpatico between what lights you up and what fills your soul. As an Aquarius, you're altruistically inclined. Your Gemini Moon adds to your intellectual approach to life, one infused with a desire to understand things that can make the world a better place.
PISCES	GEMINI	Your Sun and Moon are in signs whose symbols feature pairs: fish for Pisces and twins for Gemini. As such, you prefer multiplicity over unilaterality. You're quite fluid, a chameleon who loves to go with the flow. You've got a powerful curiosity focused on understanding subtleties.

CHAPTER 15

CANCER

SYMBOL

The Crab, a sea- and land-dwelling animal known for its hard protective shell that encases its soft interior.

ELEMENT

Water, characterized by fluidity, emotionality, reflection, and nonlinear understanding.

PLANETARY RULER

The Moon, which represents emotions, maternal instincts, and the cyclical nature of life.

MODALITY

Cardinal, which prizes initiation, ambition, and being enterprising.

136

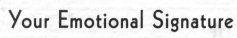

Your Emotional Signature

As the Moon symbolizes instinctive feelings, the sign in which it resides gives us more awareness about the nuances of our emotional nature. Knowing this can help us discern our essential needs, strengthen our superpowers, and be aware of our kryptonite (personal habits that can be challenging).

YOUR ESSENTIAL NEEDS

✳ *Feeling at Home*

You love having a cozy abode where you can rest and nest, retreat and renew. Your home is so important to you, and it shows. It doesn't even have to be fancy; just as long as you're surrounded by your creature comforts and its spirit reflects the care you put into it, you're happy. It just needs to radiate homey: whether through a comfy couch, bric-a-brac with sentimental value, and/or the aromas of food cooking in the kitchen. For many Cancer Moons, their home isn't important just for them: it's the place in which they gather with those they cherish, their family of origin and/or choice. When it comes to your relationship with home, it's not just the physical structure that's important to you—it's also the feeling that's essential. Wherever you go, you strive to feel at home, experiencing both a sense of security as well as belonging.

✳ *Being Part of a Family*

Cancer is the sign of the family, and for those with this Moon sign, connecting with a clan is of utmost importance. Feeling that you are part of a tribe with shared roots lends a sense of security and belonging. Surrounding yourself with people who have known you over time and upon whom you can depend can be really comforting. This familial connection, though, doesn't need to be limited to your family of origin. It may be that it's your family of choice, those not biologically related to you but who serve as your support system, who provide you that sense of feeling at home. In addition to your connections with immediate kith and kin, you may find yourself really interested in genealogy. By learning more about your ancestors, you can gain clarity into family dynamics, as well as further understand how you are both similar to and different from your relatives.

✳ *Expressing Your Emotions*

As the first water sign in the zodiac, Cancer is connected to a fountain of feelings. You have a deep reservoir of emotions that need acknowledgement and tending. Sometimes, as if out of nowhere, a swell of emotions may emerge and the next thing you know, a mood captures you and it seems like it just won't let go. Given that feelings are anything but rational, instead of fighting this current, allow yourself to flow with it, seeing where this sea of sentiments takes you and what it reveals. Often, what it may expose is whether you are feeling nourished and if your needs are being met. Actually, the importance of attending to your needs cannot be overstated. For those with Cancer Moons, acknowledging that you have them, declaring what they are, and making choices to allow for them to be satisfied is elemental to happiness and emotional well-being.

YOUR SUPERPOWERS

✷ *Caring Nature*

You're such a Mama Bear, driven to feed, nourish, and protect those that you cherish. For this, others really treasure you. In your presence, they feel safe and well taken care of. They sense that you're really interested in their emotional well-being. You express your concern in a multitude of ways: it may be through your cooking, your propensity to lend a helping hand, and/or your open-door policy that helps people feel that you're available to listen to them whenever they're in need of it.

✷ *Entertaining Skills*

You love feeding people, making sure they are nourished body, mind, and soul. You adore communing with others, notably when that involves sharing a meal. Whether it's gathering around a table or a campfire, you've got the cooking chops (or take-out know-how) to cater to your guests' needs in a way that has them feel they've won the dinner-party lottery. And that's not even taking into consideration your flair for decorating, choosing the perfect serving pieces, and your mad playlist-making skills.

✷ *Intuition*

You're really tuned in. As a sensitive soul, it's like you can read the currents around you as well as the waves of feelings that others are experiencing. This gives you quite an intuitive capacity, a powerful resource that can forge your ability to nourish yourself and create a life path that is really nurturing. Additionally, trusting your gut is a talent you can channel as you seek to help others, something inherently important to you.

YOUR KRYPTONITE

Wistfulness

You have such a strong appreciation for the past that at times you can become overly attached to it. This longing can shower you with sadness and also pull you away from truly living in the present moment. That's not to say that you should avoid being nostalgic. After all, reflecting on joyful events and having grief when experiencing loss is natural and healthy. Just be careful that you don't let the past have a pincer grip on your being able to be present *in* the present.

Subjectivity

While your sensitivity is one of your strengths, sometimes you may be so immersed in your emotions that you lose your objectivity. This may be especially true when you fear that someone or something you cherish is threatened, and you instinctively jump into Mama Bear mode. Excessive subjectivity may then shroud your clarity and ability to see situations from a wide range of angles. As you honor your feelings, also leave space for seeing things from other vantage points.

Indirectness

Crabs are known to move in an indirect fashion, scuttling sideways here and there until they finally reach their destination. Like that sidling creature—your Moon sign's totem—you may often proceed along indirect routes, given that you find moving circuitously comforting as it allows you to ascertain how you feel moment to moment. Yet, it can also cause delays and leave people wondering about your intentions. While you should move however feels right, communicating your preferred pace to others from the outset may help to ease potential frustrations.

Your Stellar Self-Care

As the Moon corresponds to our physical body as well as what we find nourishing, the sign of its placement gives us insights into how to best take care of ourselves. Here you'll find nurturing strategies, tips to overcome what causes you stress, and a health focus to pay attention to.

NURTURING STRATEGIES

✳ *The Power of Water*

You're in your element when you're in the water, which is a wonderful thing since the aqueous can have amazing healing benefits. Baths can be the perfect time-out, a way to get away from the day's demands. And if you add Epsom salts and your favorite essential oils, bathing can have additional salutary effects. Don't have a tub? Don't worry—just fill a basin with warm water and enjoy a relaxing foot soak. When you have muscle aches or pains, another way to engage the therapeutic potential of water is through contrast hydrotherapy. In this practice, you alternate between immersing the affected part of your body in hot and cold water. Doing so is thought to promote healing by enhancing blood and lymph circulation.

✳ *Turning to the Past*

You prize traditions and have a penchant for the past. Things that have stood the test of time have special appeal to you. As such, you may find a special kinship with folk remedies. Whether these are the herbs or foods that your parents and grandparents relied upon or those from cultures to which you feel an affinity, adding these to your self-care repertoire can be a boon to your betterment. Speaking of food, collecting and cooking recipes that you've inherited from your family can be quite a nourishing activity. Another means by which you can turn to the past for healing is Systemic Family Constellations, a therapeutic approach that can help to uncover multigenerational family dynamics and release the binds that they may have on you.

✳ *Honoring Cyclicity*

Cancer is ruled by the Moon, and just like Luna, which continually moves through different phases, your sign is known for its cyclical nature. This may help to explain why your moods, sexual drive, and even sleep needs may wax and wane. Understanding your cycles is therefore instrumental for shepherding your health. To do so, in a journal or calendar, track the ups and downs of different realms of your well-being—the ones previously mentioned or those that you know waver over time. After a while, see what patterns emerge, customizing your self-care approach accordingly. For example, if it's harder to fall asleep around Full Moons, wind down earlier than you usually do. Or if you realize you're always more emotionally sensitive on Mondays, schedule activities accordingly.

STRESS SPOTLIGHT

✳ *The Need to Belong*

Experiencing a sense of belonging is essential to those with Cancer Moons. Feeling part of a tribe—whether it's your family, friend group, or even the country in which you live—is key to your happiness. As such, when you feel disconnected from others, it can cause distress and upset. Even an acute situation—like your relatives not taking your ideas for the holiday gathering seriously—can leave you uneasy. Additionally, for those who have a challenging family, a lack of kinship can really disturb your sense of inner peace. To experience feeling the nurturing that comes through being part of a group, you may find yourself seeking out kindred souls whom you can call family. If you're looking for a flower essence to help you connect to a deep sense of belonging, consider Sweet Pea.

HEALTH FOCUS

✳ *Stomach*

It makes sense that the stomach is one of the areas ruled by your Moon sign. After all, Cancer is associated with nourishment, and the stomach is where the process of digestion begins in earnest. Additionally, with your intuitive and emotional orientation, trusting your gut is quite important. Stomach acid plays a key role in the digestive process, and having either too much or too little is something that can have a big impact on your well-being.

Gastroesophageal reflux disease (GERD) can lead to heartburn or acid indigestion. It occurs when acid flows upward from the stomach into the esophagus, another part of the body ruled by your Moon sign. If you have GERD—and given that a formidable number of people deal with it, you'd be in good company—know that there are certain lifestyle adjustments that can be beneficial. Smoking, eating large meals late at night, coffee, and acidic foods have been found to be triggers; see if avoiding these mollifies your symptoms. Deglycyrrhizinated licorice (DGL), bromelain, and slippery elm are herbs thought to be helpful. Also, while excess stomach acid can be problematic, so can insufficient amounts, as it leads to malabsorption of nutrients like protein and vitamin B12. Gentian and other bitter herbs may be helpful for encouraging gastric acid production.

Your Sun + Your Moon

Now that you know more about your Moon sign, it's interesting to think about it in relationship with your Sun sign. As these two luminaries are at the foundation of our essential sense of self, looking at your Sun and Moon as a pair can give you additional insights to further understand yourself. Below you will find the twelve pairings associated with the Cancer Moon.

☀ + ☾		PROFILE
ARIES	CANCER	You're a self-starter who can be a courageous advocate for your and others' needs. When it comes to the way you proceed through life, you have two different styles: with an Aries Sun you can be fast and direct, while with a Cancer Moon you often like to proceed slowly and in a circuitous manner.
TAURUS	CANCER	Feeling a sense of security is really important and has you motivated to safeguard your emotions and possessions. You're sensitive to your surroundings and want your home to be a comforting abode. With a sensually oriented Taurus Sun and a nurturing Cancer Moon, you love to cook and/or enjoy sumptuous meals.
GEMINI	CANCER	You're a blend of curiosity and sensitivity, powered by both your mind and heart. Oftentimes, you may find yourself drawn to playing a mother role to your friends or siblings. With your Gemini Sun, you love to learn. And with your Cancer Moon, much of what captures your interest may the subjects of home and family.
CANCER	CANCER	As a double Cancer, it's important for you to proceed at a slow pace; doing so gives you the space to welcome and process your powerful emotions. Whether it's gardening, cooking, or doing DIY decorative projects, you're drawn to activities that enhance your home and your ability to nourish others.
LEO	CANCER	You care a lot about people. With your Cancer Moon, you are sensitive to their needs, while with your Leo Sun, you want them to shine. Your wellspring of emotions can power your creative projects. Children, even if you don't have any of your own, may play an important role in your life.

☀ + ☾ PROFILE

VIRGO	**CANCER**	You're known for your dedication and devotion. It's important for you to be in service to others, helping them to feel their very best. With a health-oriented Virgo Sun and a sensitive Cancer Moon, it's clear to you that only by honoring your emotions can you experience optimal well-being.
LIBRA	**CANCER**	You have a knack for creating beautiful environments and organizing gatherings that cater to people's needs. With an apt-to-compromise Libra Sun and a move-indirectly Cancer Moon, it's important to be aware when being conflict avoidant can stand in your way of getting what you need.
SCORPIO	**CANCER**	With a very protective nature, you have an instinctive tendency to defend both yourself and others. At times you love when things are stirred up, while at other moments it interferes with your need for placidity. With a passionate Scorpio Sun and sensitive Cancer Moon, you're a deep-feeling creature.
SAGITTARIUS	**CANCER**	You love traveling and also love returning home. When on a journey, you have an instinctive sense of the places and activities that will feel the most nourishing. With a broad-minded Sagittarius Sun and an emotional Cancer Moon, you have both a philosophical and instinctive approach to life.
CAPRICORN	**CANCER**	You're skilled at creating structures that have people feel that they belong. As your work and family life are both important, finding a balance between the two is key. You're drawn to be a provider—of the financial support your Capricorn Sun treasures and of the emotional support your Cancer Moon prizes.
AQUARIUS	**CANCER**	You care about humanity as well as those close to you. You have a great appreciation for approaches infused with tradition as well as those steeped in innovation. Finding ways to honor both your Cancer Moon's need for closeness and your Aquarius Sun's need for distance is important to your well-being.
PISCES	**CANCER**	Your inner life is quite rich. It's your sanctuary, the place you go for inspiration as well as when you need to escape the demands of life. You've got a caring spirit and readily give of yourself to others. With your empathetic Pisces Sun and your emotional Cancer Moon, you're known for your kindness and compassion.

CHAPTER 16

LEO

SYMBOL

The Lion, an animal known for its fierceness, nobility, and magnificent roar.

ELEMENT

Fire, characterized by the dynamic energy of inspiration, enthusiasm, and passion.

144

PLANETARY RULER

The Sun, which represents vitality, creative life force, and a person's essence.

MODALITY

Fixed, which prizes reliability, predictability, and stamina.

Your Emotional Signature

As the Moon symbolizes instinctive feelings, the sign in which it resides gives us more awareness about the nuances of our emotional nature. Knowing this can help us discern our essential needs, strengthen our superpowers, and be aware of our kryptonite (personal habits that can be challenging).

YOUR ESSENTIAL NEEDS

✴ *Being Acknowledged*

It's important for you to be seen and recognized for the unique person that you are. Whether it's being appreciated for one of your special qualities or lauded for something you've created, having others offer you kudos is important. It's not that you necessarily need people circling around you, showering you with compliments all the time. While sometimes you do like to feel center stage, at other times, when shyness prevails, it's not your most favorite spot. Though you appreciate praise, it doesn't need to be extensive. Simple accolades now and then also make you happy, as they consistently remind you that people understand the value that you bring and the special person that you are. As a social creature, when others see your radiance it allows you to more boldly engage in relationships and more vibrantly radiate who you are in the world.

✴ *Loving and Being Loved*

Leo rules the heart, both the organ whose beating rhythm sustains life and the emblematic symbol that represents love. And while love stories, rom-coms, and romantic poetry may delight you, you also strive to live a life filled with ardor and adoration. Reflecting this, being the object of someone's affection is exceptionally nurturing for you, as is adoring someone so much that the mere thought of them makes your heart proverbially skip a beat. You're an inveterate romantic who is nourished not only when you are showered with attention, but also when you get to lavish it upon others. If every day was Valentine's Day—filled with amorous gestures, flowers, and chocolate—you'd be quite satisfied. Your desire for endearing relationships is broad and not just limited to an intimate partner; you adore being openhearted with others, be it your family, friends, children, or colleagues.

✴ *Maintaining Your Dignity*

Leo is the sign of royalty, and for those who have their Moon here, maintaining a sense of dignity is of the utmost importance. After all, yours is the sign of the queen and king, not the fool. While you have a creative spirit that wants to express itself, you carry within you a heightened level of self-consciousness, which acts as a guardrail to keep you from actions that may be embarrassing. Avoiding awkward situations is imperative for your maintaining a sense of nobility and confidence, qualities inherently important to you. Even if you've been working hard to hatch a plan, if you perceive that sharing it will lead to having egg on your face, you'll restrain yourself from doing so. As you've likely experienced, sometimes pride can actually get in the way of joy. After all, being too guarded may dampen your self-expression and the freedom you feel to truly be who you are.

YOUR SUPERPOWERS

✳ *Generosity*

People see you as bighearted, someone who has a courageous and magnanimous spirit. As you know firsthand how amazing it feels to be cherished, you're apt to readily show your appreciation for people you care about. You have a great capacity to give and to gift. Your seamless ability to offer your resources to others—whether your time, energy, or money—helps them to feel like they are special and that they matter.

✳ *Creativity*

You're deeply creative. It's essential for you to take your inner inspirations and use them as *prima materia* to bring things to life. Giving birth to ideas, inspirations, or even children is a generative act that speaks to your soul. You are always looking for ways to put your individual stamp on projects, as doing so is fun, rewarding, and energizing. Whether it's the way you dress, how you decorate your space, or the artistic ventures you undertake, you do it with a flair that's uniquely your own.

✳ *Charisma*

Others are quite attracted to your warmth of spirit and how you bring your heart to all you do. You've got a magical charm that radiates from deep within you, some of which may derive from the childlike wonder through which you navigate the world. Others find it captivating, as it reminds them of the power of youth and the rewards of an unjaded perspective. You prize playfulness, love fun, and invite in levity—who wouldn't find that magnetically appealing?

YOUR KRYPTONITE

✳ *Pride*

While maintaining your dignity is really important to you, at times it can be an obstacle to sourcing the unfettered joy you love to feel. After all, if you're averse to trying new things for fear of embarrassment, it could leave you feeling stifled, not freely able to express your thoughts and feelings. Of course, while it's important for you to feel proud, try not to let pride get in your way of sharing yourself—and your gifts—with others.

✳ *Melodrama*

With your Moon in Leo, you've got a theatrical side, which often infuses itself into the way you express your emotions, peppering them with exuberance and passion. While this may serve you well, a challenge can arise when you're frustrated: your fiery feelings may erupt and melodrama may take center stage, potentially causing others to not take your sentiments as seriously as they should. It's not that you should hide your feelings—just be aware of how their delivery impacts your audience.

✳ *Self-Orientation*

Your Moon sign takes many clues from its planetary ruler, the Sun, including a desire to sometimes feel at the center of things. Of course, while having a well-developed ego is important as it can amplify your confidence to meet challenges, an overactive need to be in the spotlight can cause issues, including upsetting relationship dynamics. While you should never dim your light, knowing when it's best to turn your brightness up or down is a skill that yields great reward.

Your Stellar Self-Care

As the Moon corresponds to our physical body as well as what we find nourishing, the sign of its placement gives us insights into how to best take care of ourselves. Here you'll find nurturing strategies, tips to overcome what causes you stress, and a health focus to pay attention to.

NURTURING STRATEGIES

✳ *Being Creative*

Those with Leo Moons see the world as their canvas, a colorful landscape in which they can express their unique selves, a place where their dreams and visions can take shape and come alive. Speaking of canvases, make sure that you have many—whether literal or figurative ones—in your life upon which you can create. Whether it's painting, singing, flower arranging, or another art form that allows you to give shape to your inspirations, activities that invite you to be generative are really nurturing. Additionally, find everyday experiences—such as cooking a meal, decorating your office, or styling your outfits—that allow you to express your personal flair. Remember you're never too old to connect to your creative self and live an artful life.

✳ *Pampering Yourself*

Caring for your well-being doesn't necessarily have to equate with sacrifice and asceticism. In fact, there are many health-supporting activities that are not only enjoyable but that will have you feeling royally pampered. The act of granting yourself permission for indulgences can itself be really nourishing. Plus, being tended to by another—whether in a massage, facial, or body treatment—suits your sybaritic self. It's possible to be a powerful agent of your well-being without needing to spend a lot of money or even go anywhere. Just dedicate a swath of time to lounge about your home, napping in the sunshine, painting your nails, giving your hair a deep-moisturizing treatment, or any other of the favorite lazy-day activities in which you love to indulge.

✳ *Being Playful*

Thinking about your wide-eyed wonder and fun-loving nature, it's no surprise that Leo is the sign associated with children. Activities that speak to your strong childlike spirit and zest for life will make your heart sing. Plus, having fun is not only your strong suit, but a surefire way to relaxation. Take the time to play games or even play on a playground. Gather some art supplies and spend time painting, or get decked out, join up with friends, and paint the town red. And, of course, connecting with kids can also be a great way to nourish your youthful essence. Whether you're mentoring them or just hanging out, spending time with children can give you a healthy dose of joy.

STRESS SPOTLIGHT

✳ *Wavering Confidence*

It's important for you to feel self-assured. You aim to have faith in yourself and confidently believe in your convictions and capabilities. Like others, though, there are times when uncertainty may plague you. When this happens and you find yourself floating through a nebula of self-doubt, no matter how loudly people sing your praises, it seems to fall on deaf ears. This can have two effects that may undermine your confidence: it may lead you to shrink from view, or have you boast a bravado that is sourced on shaky ground. Strategies to practice that can enhance your self-appreciation include making an inventory of your achievements, treasuring the special gifts you have, and challenging the negative thoughts you hold. For a flower essence that can help you have more confidence in your competence, and really hear others when they speak about the gifts and talents you have, consider Larch.

HEALTH FOCUS

✳ *Spine*

It makes sense that the spine is one of the realms of the body ruled by Leo. After all, with your Moon in the sign associated with confidence, formidable resolve, and strength of character, you're known for your strong backbone. Plus, with the Sun as Leo's ruler, your Moon sign is associated with vitality and vigor. Consequently, in yogic wisdom traditions, one of the main channels through which life force energy (known as *prana*) travels is the spine.

There are many ways to strengthen your spine's well-being, including maintaining a healthy weight and ensuring that your diet gives you adequate amounts of bone-building nutrients. Upholding proper posture is important and can be aided by key ergonomic considerations, such as using a lumbar-support pillow when driving, and having your computer monitor at eye level. There are also numerous yoga poses thought to increase the mobility of the spine, including Cobra, Boat, and Downward-Facing Dog. Additionally, there's kundalini yoga, a practice that includes breathing exercises, physical poses, and mantra chanting, all aimed to foster the flow of life force energy through the spine. Together with its traditional benefits of enhanced awareness, research suggests that kundalini yoga reduces stress, builds resilience, and enhances cognitive function.

Your Sun + Your Moon

Now that you know more about your Moon sign, it's interesting to think about it in relationship with your Sun sign. As these two luminaries are at the foundation of our essential sense of self, looking at your Sun and Moon as a pair can give you additional insights to further understand yourself. Below you will find the twelve pairings associated with the Leo Moon.

☀ + ☾		PROFILE
ARIES	**LEO**	You've got unbounded energy and teem with excitement. While you're happy to do your own thing, getting recognition for your achievements is something you always appreciate. With a self-starting Aries Sun and self-expressive Leo Moon, you're a pioneer when it comes to creativity.
TAURUS	**LEO**	Slow and steady wins the race—that is, as long as you have the latitude to be yourself along the way. While you try to be diligent when it comes to your resources, sometimes your generosity leaves you a bit overextended. It's important to pay homage to both your practical Taurus side and your fun-loving Leo Moon.
GEMINI	**LEO**	Your mind is bright and you want to be recognized for your unique perspectives. You have a flair for infusing your words with artistry and sometimes even drama. With your Gemini Sun, you're a polymath with numerous interests. Given your Moon is in Leo, it's important people see this as a valuable asset.
CANCER	**LEO**	You love taking care of others as it lights you up and feels like part of your raison d'être. It fills your heart to be generous with those you love. With your demure Cancer Sun and radiant Leo Moon, sometimes you like to do your magic from behind the scenes, and sometimes in clear view.
LEO	**LEO**	As a double Leo, you have a generous spirit and skill for finding situations that allow you to share your heart's wishes. You seek out experiences that have you feeling like you're the king or queen of your realm. Your playfulness and childlike spirit are some of the qualities by which people know you.

☀ + ☾		PROFILE
VIRGO ♍	**LEO** ♌	When you marry your eye for detailed precision with your artistic flair, you can be a master at crafting unique solutions. Find ways to honor both your Virgo Sun's desire for organization and your Leo Moon's need for creative freedom. Just don't hold yourself to too high standards or it will stifle your ability to express yourself.
LIBRA ♎	**LEO** ♌	Social relationships really brighten your life. Gathering with friends gives you joy, and if there's delicious food and an artful environment, all the better. When you bring your Leo Moon generosity to the alliances that your Libra Sun so cherishes, everyone wins and feels special.
SCORPIO ♏	**LEO** ♌	You love when people recognize your ability to solve mysteries. Giving yourself the freedom to boldly own your desires is a key to your happiness. With a Scorpio Sun, you may want to hide your deep feelings, and yet with an expressive Leo Moon, sometimes it may be challenging to keep things under wraps.
SAGITTARIUS ♐	**LEO** ♌	You love feeling inspired and are enthusiastic about sharing your discoveries with others. Traveling brings out your playful side. As a Sagittarius Sun, your beliefs are important to you. With a Leo Moon, you've got a knack for sharing them creatively and with the unique flair for which you are known.
CAPRICORN ♑	**LEO** ♌	You're the kind of person who could build an empire dedicated to sharing the things you love. Sometimes, though, your Capricorn judiciousness and Leo Moon playfulness can clash. Finding outlets that allow you to be both your hardworking and fun-loving self is key to discovering more joy.
AQUARIUS ♒	**LEO** ♌	You love when you can contribute your creative talents to a collective project. It makes your heart sing when you can be yourself and also part of something larger than yourself. With an Aquarius Sun, you like to march to the beat of your own drum, and with a Leo Moon, you don't mind if people applaud you for this.
PISCES ♓	**LEO** ♌	With a poetic Pisces Sun and an expressive Leo Moon, you're a visionary who dreams in color, an artist who taps their imagination for creative inspiration. While you're naturally sensitive to others, what sometimes stands in your way of being fully empathetic is when you feel that doing so will make you invisible.

CHAPTER 17

VIRGO

SYMBOL

The Maiden, an icon of purity, fertility, and sacred commitment.

ELEMENT

Earth, characterized by the grounded energy of creativity, resilience, and practicality.

PLANETARY RULER

Mercury, which represents the mind, communication, and language.

MODALITY

Mutable, which prizes flexibility, adaptability, and movement.

152

Your Emotional Signature

As the Moon symbolizes instinctive feelings, the sign in which it resides gives us more awareness about the nuances of our emotional nature. Knowing this can help us discern our essential needs, strengthen our superpowers, and be aware of our kryptonite (personal habits that can be challenging).

YOUR ESSENTIAL NEEDS

✳ *Striving for Cleanliness*

Virgo Moons place a very high value on their environment being neat and tidy. For some, this manifests as a tireless effort to clean, with an instinctive urge to immediately pick up after yourself as well as others (that is, if your marked efforts fail to encourage your family or roommates to straighten up). And yet there are others with this Moon placement whose abodes have more of a "bless this mess" vibe; it's not that they don't crave cleanliness, but rather they may feel paralyzed when imagining all the work it takes to achieve it. A need for pristine can also show up in your hygiene routine, with a strong urge to wash your hands after every outing and/or to shower immediately after exercise, sex, or gardening. You know that saying "cleanliness is close to godliness"? That idiom likely was coined by someone with a Virgo Moon.

✳ *Being Organized*

It's not just cleanliness that Virgo Moons extol, as you also need things to be organized. And with your natural inclination to deify details, it's not only that you hate when things are out of order—you actually enjoy the process of putting things in their place. To you, there's something really satisfying about classifying your spices by cuisine, alphabetizing your books by author, and color-coding pantry items by use-by date that's hard to explain to others. Although they do get to experience the benefits of your organizational process: after all, you are the one they call when they want tips on streamlining their filing system, embarking upon meal planning, or creating a spreadsheet to manage their budget. When your space is free of clutter, it's easy for your mind to be as well. This allows you to be more efficient, something you also prize, saving you time so you can focus on other more important tasks.

153

✳ *Feeling Healthy*

With your striving for purity, love of efficacy, and interest in how systems work, your Moon sign is the one most often associated with health consciousness. And, as an earth sign connected with the harvest, Virgo appreciates natural foods and how they can be a foundation of self-care. You're apt to consider your well-being from a holistic perspective. It's obvious to you that an issue you experience in one part of the body may cause a symptom to appear in another. After all, you're naturally inclined to see how seemingly disparate parts relate to one another and constitute essential elements of the whole. With your vigilance for details and your penchant for perfection, noticing even the slightest thing awry may exacerbate acute worry as well as hypochondrial notions. While it's important for you to honor your desire to feel your very best, try to do so without sliding into excess worry about your health.

YOUR SUPERPOWERS

✳ *Problem Solving*

You love finding solutions to problems large and small, with your skills for being able to effectively do so deriving from your multiple talents. You're quite keen on seeing when things are out of place, and therefore you've got a knack for identifying the existence of predicaments. As a critical thinker, you are able to perceive multiple distinct answers and then work though in your mind which one may hold the key to cutting any Gordian knot.

✳ *Artisanship*

You're instinctively drawn to using your hands to create functional objects that will make your life more efficient and enjoyable. And with your eye for detail, affinity for refinement, and deftness at organization, you can be the master of any craft that inspires you. Remember that being an artisan doesn't necessarily have to equate with traditional handicrafts like knitting, sewing, or jewelry making. You may just as likely flex your creative muscle by decorating your home, cooking, or gardening.

✳ *Planning*

Given you're quite fond of things being orderly, another craft you've mastered is that of planning. No matter the destination, whether literal or metaphorical, you are gifted in being able to readily figure out the road map that will get you there. Your penchant for planning isn't just due to it letting you express your consummate organizational skills. It's also because it serves another important purpose: working out the details beforehand gives you a sense of greater control, which can reduce your propensity to worry that things won't work out.

 YOUR KRYPTONITE

✳ *Being Critical*

You've got an inclination for wanting things to be the best they can. While this can be laudable, combined with your eye for precision, this tendency can sometimes be so all-consuming that it leaves you swirling in judgment. A key to curtailing the urge to criticize is compassion: remind yourself that people—including yourself—do the very best they can at any given moment. Also, don't lose sight of the fact that while perfection may be ideal, it is only an ideal, not a reality.

✳ *Worry*

While you attend to numerous details to ensure that things go right, you have an unmatched ability to imagine all the ways that they can also go wrong. When your apprehension is elevated, it can get the best of you, causing negative thinking to invade the many corners of your mind. In addition to trying to manage your expectations, other ways to reduce the propensity to worry include getting regular exercise, engaging in a meditation practice, and talking about your concerns to others.

✳ *Lack of Spontaneity*

Being a natural planner helps you keep things organized and orderly. Although, if you're overly attached to a schedule of what should happen when, it can stymie your spontaneity and create undue stress when sudden changes do occur. Honor your need to plan as well as a desire to invite in the impromptu: block out free periods of time on your calendar, letting yourself do whatever it is that you're drawn to in the moment.

Your Stellar Self-Care

As the Moon corresponds to our physical body as well as what we find nourishing, the sign of its placement gives us insights into how to best take care of ourselves. Here you'll find nurturing strategies, tips to overcome what causes you stress, and a health focus to pay attention to.

NURTURING STRATEGIES

✳ *Cleansing and Purifying*

Those with Virgo Moons have an affinity for purity. They like things, including themselves, to be clean and pristine. While numerous activities will support you in this aim, one of the most holistic places to start is with what you eat. Opt for a whole-foods diet that contains minimal processed foods—ideally organically grown and humanely raised. It will provide you with a bounty of nutrients while not causing your liver to work too hard to detoxify synthetic substances. Another great way to feel cleansed is to ensure you're adequately hydrated, drinking about eight glasses of filtered water each day.

✳ *Being of Service*

As Virgo is inspired by making things better while also closely associated with being of service, you may find yourself drawn to wanting to help improve the lives of others. Those with this Moon placement have a very strong charitable side; when they actively assist others, it leaves them feeling really nourished. There are many ways you can make a difference in other people's lives: working at a soup kitchen, advocating for the rights of the underprivileged, planting trees, or fostering a pet being just a few ideas. Not only is volunteering fulfilling but it's been found to be salutary to well-being, including reducing stress and enhancing cognitive function.

✳ *Feeling Supported by Nature*

As an earth sign, Virgo has a heightened sensitivity to the natural world. As such, you may find spending time in the outdoors to be quite rewarding. When you can, ditch the gym and exercise outside instead. And when the weather aligns, pack a picnic and head to the park or seaside. As an alternative or adjunct to your usual mindfulness practice, go outside and meditate in nature; for example, when doing a breath meditation, tune into the trees, and as you focus on your exhalations and inhalations, sense how you are doing so in coordination with them. And given yours is the sign of the harvest, growing some of your own food—even if just windowsill herbs—is a great way to feel more grounded in your well-being.

STRESS SPOTLIGHT

✳ *Perfectionist Streak*

With your methodical mind and critical eye, you're always seeking ways to improve things and work hard to that end. Although, when your perfectionist nature gets involved, good is often not good enough, and your potential to criticize emerges. In turn, you end up faulting yourself—or others—for perceived mistakes or shortcomings, stirring up worry, stress, and upset. It's important to remember that while the act of perfecting may be laudable, perfection itself is an illusion, a false benchmark that when held as a goal can only lead to a path of perturbation. While the need to have things fine-tuned is part of your nature, try to do so without setting unrealistic ideals against which you judge yourself or others. If you'd like a flower essence that can inspire tolerance and help you release your critical edge, try Beech.

HEALTH FOCUS

✳ *Digestive System*

As Virgo is the sign associated with discernment and assimilation, it's no surprise that it governs the digestive system in general and the small intestines in particular. The important role that the gut plays in our health cannot be overstated. It's where nutrient absorption and waste elimination occur. Plus, owing to its widespread neurological network, it's now thought of as the "second brain." This has led researchers to believe it plays a role in both our physical health and emotional well-being.

If you're sensitive to certain compounds like gluten, it may cause flare-ups in your small intestines. Should you notice that you get unwelcome symptoms—such as brain fog, flatulence, or reduced energy—when you eat certain foods, consider going on a modified elimination diet, with guidance from your doctor. For two weeks, remove suspicious foods and then slowly reintroduce them one by one, tracking whether any cause unwanted symptoms. Consuming adequate fiber is key to maintaining digestive health, as is eating a diet rich in anti-inflammatory nutrients, such as omega-3 fatty acids as well as the flavonoid and carotenoid phytonutrients concentrated in fruits and vegetables. Your gut health is another reason to try to stem your worry, since it can tie the stomach in knots, leading to not only distress but the inhibition of digestion.

Your Sun + Your Moon

Now that you know more about your Moon sign, it's interesting to think about it in relationship with your Sun sign. As these two luminaries are at the foundation of our essential sense of self, looking at your Sun and Moon as a pair can give you additional insights to further understand yourself. Below you will find the twelve pairings associated with the Virgo Moon.

☀ + ☾		PROFILE
ARIES	**VIRGO**	You're instinctive and methodical. You can sometimes feel frustrated when your Virgo Moon's need for precision dampens your Aries Sun's need to quickly move on to the next activity. Find ways to honor your passionate and analytical nature so you can be a fervent champion lit up by being in service to others.
TAURUS	**VIRGO**	You've got a strong practical streak and a no-nonsense way of dealing with things. You also have an inherent alliance with nature, finding it to be a haven of comfort. Your Taurus Sun loves being surrounded with beautiful objects, and if they're also functional, your Virgo Moon is quite happy.
GEMINI	**VIRGO**	As a Gemini, communication is key for you. And, thanks to your Virgo Moon, you place a high prize on information that's both organized and precise. It's important to you to have an instrument—be it words or built forms—that you can sculpt, capable of efficiently delivering messages you deem important.
CANCER	**VIRGO**	You're like a baker; you extol precision and love following recipes to create things that will nourish and benefit others. Dedicated and devoted, you're handy around the house and love to fix family problems. Your Virgo Moon instinctively tries to problem-solve any challenge that your emotional Cancer Sun experiences.
LEO	**VIRGO**	You have an appreciation for both artists and artisans. You embody a special brand of kindness that comes from your Leo Sun's generosity and your Virgo Moon's affinity for being of service. Sometimes you like to shine while at other moments you're more demure. Allowing both adequate expression is key.

☀ + ☾		PROFILE
VIRGO	**VIRGO**	You're a master craftsperson, who loves a good fixer-upper. As a double Virgo, you've got an eagle eye for recognizing what needs mending and a passion for remedying it. Serious about your health, you're exceptionally connected to the systems and routines that can enhance it.
LIBRA	**VIRGO**	To you, beauty needs to not only have aesthetic properties but functional ones as well. Between your socially fluent Libra Sun and your methodological Virgo Moon, you're skilled at negotiating and crafting agreements. You have a great appreciation for those who can teach you tricks of the trade to be more organized.
SCORPIO	**VIRGO**	You are attracted to mysteries and love to solve them. With your persevering Scorpio Sun and your analytical Virgo Moon, you'll leave no stone unturned as you pursue your passion projects. You're drawn to crafting formulas that will allow you to further understand your deeply emotional nature.
SAGITTARIUS	**VIRGO**	When you embark upon the journeys that your Sagittarius Sun adores, it's important to make sure you do so in an organized and efficient manner. After all, your Virgo Moon is a stickler for details. Being able to see the parts that make up the whole is one of your strong suits.
CAPRICORN	**VIRGO**	No matter what you do, you're a master architect. Your Virgo Moon pays attention to the details of every blueprint while your Capricorn Sun works hard to envision solutions of lasting value. As both of your luminaries are in earth signs, you're grounded and practical, displaying a strong kinship with nature.
AQUARIUS	**VIRGO**	You want to make the world a better place. You're focused upon social progress and bent on improving things. With your Aquarian skill of pattern recognition and your Virgoan ability to see how the parts fit together, you have a strong interest in how things are connected.
PISCES	**VIRGO**	Your Virgo Moon can ground the imagination of your Pisces Sun, helping you give shape and form to your dreams. Your organizational skills and intuitive know-how are a powerful combo when it comes to envisioning solutions and resolutions. Your idealism can move mountains while at times can also lead to disillusionment.

CHAPTER 18

LIBRA

SYMBOL

The Scales, an object symbolizing justice, harmony, balance, and equality.

ELEMENT

Air, characterized by the agile energy of observation, logic, and sociability.

PLANETARY RULER

Venus, which represents love, beauty, and the force of attraction.

MODALITY

Cardinal, which prizes initiation, ambition, and being enterprising.

Your Emotional Signature

As the Moon symbolizes instinctive feelings, the sign in which it resides gives us more awareness about the nuances of our emotional nature. Knowing this can help us discern our essential needs, strengthen our superpowers, and be aware of our kryptonite (personal habits that can be challenging).

YOUR ESSENTIAL NEEDS

✳ *Surrounding Yourself with Beauty*

With Venus as your sign's planetary sovereign, it follows that beauty deeply nourishes your soul. It's important for your environment to be filled with beautiful things that bring you delight. For you, it's not just what's in the space that's important but also how it's arranged. A sense of balance and harmony is key, and you've got an uncanny ability to perceive when there's incongruity and something is amiss. Your attraction to splendor extends beyond your environs, encompassing your love of luxury and the finer things in life. The subject of beauty itself interests you, and you ascribe to the maxim that it is in the eye of the beholder, curious to understand what others find alluring. Having conversations about aesthetic matters not only allows you to deepen your social connections but gives you further understanding of this most important and engaging subject.

✳ *Being in Relationships*

Libra is one of the most social and convivial signs in the zodiac. And with your Moon located there, the time you share with others—and the discoveries that doing so yields—are enriching beyond measure. While you, of course, can find joy on your own, you also have a sense that certain things can only be realized through the magic that occurs when people share an experience together. And while you're an equal-opportunity social butterfly who can have fun in groups, it's in one-on-one relationships that you find the most pleasure. Your reverence for partnership extends to your professional life as well, as you'd much rather work with others than in isolation. Not only does it make it more interesting and lead to additional creative breakthroughs, but it gives you another opportunity to build the social bonds so important to your life.

✳ *Prizing Equality*

With the symbol for your Moon sign being the scales, it's no surprise that equality and fairness are paramount. When things are balanced, it feels good, and when you perceive them to be off-kilter, so are you. You've got a knack for calibration—which itself has the word *libra* embedded within it—and great skill in assessing whether something has parity as well as creating measures to bring things back to balance. You place a lot of attention on ensuring that things are equitable; for example, you'll try to spend equal time with each of your closest friends, and worry if you don't allocate your resources uniformly among your children or your nieces and nephews. Your need for things to be just may not solely be limited to the sphere of your personal life. Likely, you're also concerned with larger-scale justice issues, whether those revolve around race, gender, and/or socioeconomics.

YOUR SUPERPOWERS

✳ *Diplomacy*

Libra is known as the diplomat of the zodiac. With your Moon there, not only do you possess a deep-seated desire for mediating resolution, but you have a flair for doing so. Holding your vision for fairness in sight, you're able to see things from numerous vantage points to help determine equitable outcomes. That you do this with tact and poise is another reason why it's often you that friends and colleagues call when mediating is in order.

✳ *Graciousness*

You have a way with people, an ability that has them feel at ease. You exhibit a natural kindness and courtesy that has others feel that you care and that they are special. And regardless of what you may be feeling—even if you're swirling inside—you usually appear calm, cool, and collected, wanting to engage with those around you. No wonder so many people consider you a friend and love spending time with you.

✳ *Trusted Counsel*

In addition to wanting to be in your company, others seek you out for your sage counsel. After all, your Libra Moon gifts you with an impeccable ability to stand back and see things from numerous angles, taking an array of factors into consideration. Add to this your interest in others and wanting to help them connect to greater grace and ease, and you're likely one of the people that they speed dial when they need some trusted advice.

YOUR KRYPTONITE

✳ *Compromise*

As an arbiter extraordinaire, you are a master at helping others make concessions to resolve a dispute. Sometimes, though, you take the notion of compromise too far, notably when it comes to yourself. After all, as someone who prizes peace, you often assume that it's you who needs to relinquish their desires for the sake of accord. As you've likely experienced numerous times, doing so is often a surefire way to inner discord. When looking for a solution that yields harmony, don't forget that you are an important part of the equation.

✳ *Indulgence*

You have a penchant for pleasure and an affinity for the finer things in life. While you love living *la bella vita*, it sometimes presents you with challenges. For example, with Libra ruling sugar, you not only have a sweet nature but a passion for sweets, which can disrupt your blood sugar balance and add on extra weight. To rein in your proclivity for indulgence, remember one of your guiding principles: the value of balance and moderation.

✳ *Indecision*

There are benefits to seeing things from various angles, and the pros and cons inherent in each. However, it also brings its own set of challenges, notably when it stymies your ability to effortlessly make choices. FOBO (the fear of a better option) is one decision-procrastinating cause. Another is the concern that your selection will upset someone. Regarding the latter, as un-Libra as it sounds, remember that you can't please everyone all the time, no matter how hard you try.

Your Stellar Self-Care

As the Moon corresponds to our physical body as well as what we find nourishing, the sign of its placement gives us insights into how to best take care of ourselves. Here you'll find nurturing strategies, tips to overcome what causes you stress, and a health focus to pay attention to.

NURTURING STRATEGIES

Being Lavish

As luxury is your love language, use your appreciation of sybaritic pleasures and beautiful treasures as a motivator to take care of yourself. Because the idea of someone pampering you is nourishing, treat yourself to a spa session now and again. Or opt instead to do a facial at home, and with the money you save, indulge in a high-quality mask or other luxurious skin-care product. Allowing yourself some dedicated "me time" to relax can also be a lavish experience if you're used to working really hard. Another idea: spring for a really good pan or essential countertop appliance as it will elevate your cooking game, inspiring you to prepare more healthy meals.

Getting Fit with Friends

As someone who is relationship oriented, you may find yourself more motivated to engage in healing activities if you can make them into a social occasion and do them with others. For example, if getting yourself into a regular fitness routine has been challenging, find a workout partner or two. Have you been wanting to try out that new natural-foods café but haven't been so keen to go there alone? Suggest it to your friends as a spot for your next Sunday brunch gathering. And, if you've been looking for inspiration to write down and reflect upon your dreams, find a friend also interested in their oneiric visions. Committing to sharing your dreams with each other on an ongoing basis will help you further tap into their fount of wisdom.

Being Romantic

With your Libra Moon, it's not just your platonic relationships that make your heart sing. After all, as a romantic who prizes partnerships, you really cherish those with whom you are in an intimate alliance. Spending time with that special someone can be really nourishing; if the activity you share is a health-supporting one, it can be a wellspring for well-being, for the both of you and for your relationship. Some ideas include practicing partner yoga, meditating together, or enjoying a couple's massage. When considering plans for your next date, instead of opting for drinks or a meal, propose something active. Whether it's a hike, taking a whirl at paddleboarding, or a night out at the roller rink, it will get you moving and also move your partnership forward.

STRESS SPOTLIGHT

✳ *Decision Making*

Being a champion for equality is one of your many calling cards, even if it's also one of the things that escalates your stress. As you seek to have things be equitable, you may weigh and measure every option, often again and again. This can consume your time, delay decision making, and leave you feeling tense. When you allocate too much of your schedule to helping others find balance, it can leave you feeling imbalanced in your life. Remember too that while each decision you make has value, should a certain choice not achieve your sought-after aims, an opportunity for a revision will likely arise. If you're looking for a flower essence to aid you in navigating through the fog of indecision, helping you to clarify your inner resolve and more quickly and confidently make decisions, try Scleranthus.

HEALTH FOCUS

✳ *Blood Sugar Balance*

In accordance with Libra's planetary ruler Venus being associated with sugar, it's also connected to our glucose levels, making blood sugar something to keep your eye on. Imbalances can disturb your physical energy and mental focus, and if left unmanaged, erratic sugar levels may lead to more serious health conditions. The good news is that while genetics may play a role, blood sugar balance can be improved through an array of lifestyle factors.

Dietary strategies are key to keeping blood sugar in check. Whole foods—such as vegetables, fruits, beans, nuts, and whole grains—contain beneficial fiber and antioxidants. You can further refine your dietary approach by looking for those that have a low glycemic index. These are the ones that are metabolized more slowly, and therefore don't lead to rapid rises in blood sugar. Additionally, consider eating several small meals throughout the day rather than larger ones spaced farther apart. And don't overlook the power of your spice rack to rack up health benefits: for example, cinnamon, fennel, rosemary, and fenugreek are suggested to have anti-diabetic properties. Maintaining optimal weight is also important for keeping blood sugar in check. Additionally, a regular fitness routine is beneficial, given that exercise helps improve cells' sensitivity to insulin, a key to balancing glucose.

Your Sun + Your Moon

Now that you know more about your Moon sign, it's interesting to think about it in relationship with your Sun sign. As these two luminaries are at the foundation of our essential sense of self, looking at your Sun and Moon as a pair can give you additional insights to further understand yourself. Below you will find the twelve pairings associated with the Libra Moon.

☀ + ☾		PROFILE
ARIES	**LIBRA**	With your Sun in warrior Aries and your Moon in fairness-oriented Libra, you love to champion beauty, pleasure, and justice. An ongoing focus for you is ensuring that you meet your needs to honor your individual spirit while also respecting your love of being in relationships.
TAURUS	**LIBRA**	With both your Taurus Sun and Libra Moon being ruled by Venus, you're a model of grace. You have a seemingly effortless ability to invite beauty, delight, and pleasure into your life. When it comes to your relationships, you are quite steady and dependable.
GEMINI	**LIBRA**	Engaging with other people helps you to learn and continue to grow. You likely have a wide social circle filled with people from different age groups and walks of life: it's one way you balance your Libra Moon's need for relationships with your Gemini Sun's desire for variety.
CANCER	**LIBRA**	Your home needs to not only be cozy but beautiful. With your Cancer Sun's caring nature and your Libra Moon's sensitivity to injustice, you may find yourself called to be the peacemaker in your family. Just watch that a tendency to sidestep perceived conflicts doesn't cause more conflict within you.
LEO	**LIBRA**	Spending time with others makes you happy. Your Leo Sun loves to have fun while your Libra Moon finds social interactions really rewarding. Identifying someone to serve as a muse for your creative projects, or doing them in collaboration with others, brings you a lot of fulfillment.

VIRGO / **LIBRA**

You've got a talent for seeing beauty; with your Virgo Sun you can appreciate the artistry inherent in details while your Libra Moon has an affinity for objects infused with aesthetic value. One of your go-to strategies for problem solving is determining a formula that brings happiness to as many people as possible.

LIBRA / **LIBRA**

As a double Libra, you are a master of cordiality who prizes partnerships and glides through life with grace and finesse. With your strong need for things to be harmonious, just watch that a propensity for being conflict avoidant doesn't get in your way of getting what you need.

SCORPIO / **LIBRA**

You love relationships that help you explore the mysteries of life. You're attracted to art that isn't only beautiful but also has deep meaning. Your Scorpio Sun likes to stir the pot while your Libra Moon wants things to be peaceful; finding a way to balance your needs for both intensity and harmony is key to your happiness.

SAGITTARIUS / **LIBRA**

Between your Sagittarius Sun's desire to savor life and your Libra Moon being nourished by sybaritic experiences, you love to have a good time. Your relationships are a vehicle through which you learn about life. And nothing feels more satisfying than traveling with a friend or exploring other cultures with your partner.

CAPRICORN / **LIBRA**

While a conscientious Capricorn, your Libra Moon ensures that you regularly carve out time from your busy work schedule to honor your need for social engagements and aesthetic pleasure. A powerful part of your ability to get things done comes from your deftness at navigating relationships.

AQUARIUS / **LIBRA**

You're intrigued by people, curious to know what makes them tick. You're inspired by relationships of all kinds and appreciate hanging out with others, whether in groups or on a one-to-one basis. As a progressive Aquarius with a fairness-oriented Libra Moon, you're interested in social justice and promoting equality.

PISCES / **LIBRA**

You love *love* and have a romantic view of life. You are guided by visions of the ideal, including when it comes to your relationships. As a compassionate Pisces with a peace-upholding Libra Moon, you need to watch your tendency of putting other people's needs ahead of your own.

CHAPTER 19

SCORPIO

SYMBOL

The Scorpion, an animal known for thriving in the dark, moving in the shadows, and protecting itself with its sting.

ELEMENT

Water, characterized by fluidity, emotionality, reflection, and nonlinear understanding.

168

PLANETARY RULERS

Mars, which represents desire, courage, self-initiation, and a call to action; and Pluto, which connects us to survival instincts, power, transformation, and the cycles of life.

MODALITY

Fixed, which prizes reliability, predictability, and stamina.

Your Emotional Signature

As the Moon symbolizes instinctive feelings, the sign in which it resides gives us more awareness about the nuances of our emotional nature. Knowing this can help us discern our essential needs, strengthen our superpowers, and be aware of our kryptonite (personal habits that can be challenging).

YOUR ESSENTIAL NEEDS

✳ *Going Deep*

While others like to glide across the surface of life, not you: you're naturally drawn to what resides below, knowing that that's where to find many of life's precious treasures. Some of the underground terrain you're called to explore resides in the emotional realm; you're extremely passionate about understanding what others are feeling. Your interest in knowing what makes people tick arises both from curiosity and self-protection. Regarding the latter, you reason that if you've taken another's emotional pulse, you feel you'll have less of a chance of being blindsided later on. When it comes to relationships, your most valued ones are those in which you can reveal your depths and your many-layered self. Owing to your lived experiences and perceptive abilities, you're able to navigate the underworld with people and hold space for them as they navigate situations that may elicit grief, sorrow, and/or fear.

✳ *Being in Control*

You love to sit in the power seat. It's the place that has you feel the safest since it allows you to readily scan your environment for both opportunities and dangers that may appear at a moment's notice. Being in control is a powerful Scorpio Moon emotional safeguarding strategy, perceived as giving you the ability to avert surprises that could catch you off guard. Also, it allows you to helm the command center and direct resources to where you feel they best belong, at the behest of your strong urge to guide forth amazing creative feats. You have an uncanny ability to have people feel that you have everything under control, even when you don't. Some of this talent comes from being a master of masking: while you're emotionally intense, you're quite skilled at shrouding your true feelings from everyone save your trusted cadres of confidants.

✳ *Having Privacy*

Sometimes you need the time and space to be on your own so that you can process all that arises from the wellspring of your emotional being. As such, having privacy, free from being observed or disturbed by others, is really nurturing. You also like to keep your private life private as this gives you a greater sense of freedom to be able to have experiences that others may not understand or align with. That said, it's not that you keep everything under lock and key; sometimes you have the desire to share intimate aspects with others, whether to those in your close circle or a wider audience. Yet when you do this, you do it strategically and with great intention; it may be for a creative purpose you deem destined to be transformative or as a means of protection, since it gives you more certainty that you'll be able to control the message.

YOUR SUPERPOWERS

✳ *Discretion*

You're a master at guarding the vault: those who want their secrets kept safe know to share them with you. People instinctively sense that you'll keep whatever they tell you under wraps given the high price you place on privacy. Your ability to be discreet can also put you in a position of power, something you find comforting. After all, while you get access to others' confidential information, since you play your cards so close to your chest, they don't necessarily have entrée to yours.

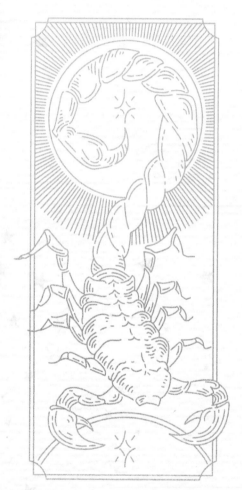

170
—

✳ *Detective Abilities*

You love to dig deep and explore what's below the surface, astute at piercing the veil and seeing what resides behind facades. This is one of the reasons that you're not only drawn to mysteries but also so adept at solving them, whether those in books, on the screen, or in your own life. Additionally, as someone who is aware that they have motivations they often shroud from others, you're more readily able to perceive and understand the range of hidden ambitions that others may possess.

✳ *Seduction*

There's an air of mystery about you, a *je ne sais quoi* that many can't put their finger on, which others find quite attractive. And even if people perceive you to be intense, this only strengthens the pull you seem to have on them and their desire to want to know or work with you. Whether or not you consciously emanate your seductive side, it still serves to influence people, drawing them closer and inspiring their desire to want to be your ally.

 YOUR KRYPTONITE

✳ *Suspicion*

It makes sense that you've got a suspicious mind. After all, you maintain that if you can so readily keep a secret, why can't others as well? When you get caught in an eddy of distrust, you could find yourself dubious of most every claim that you encounter. Not only is this stressful but it can have you feeling really isolated. To try to break this cycle, continually remind yourself that sometimes people actually do say what they mean and mean what they say.

✳ *Going to Extremes*

With your love of the intense and your all-or-nothing bent, you tend to go to extremes. And while this may contribute to your capacity of endurance, it can sometimes be taxing if it has you exhaust your time, energy, or resources. Of course, you won't—and shouldn't—completely stop exploring the edges. Just be more mindful about going there. When you feel pulled to pull out all the stops, see whether stopping yourself may bring you someplace that would better serve you.

✳ *Stirring the Pot*

You don't mind when things get a little messy; after all, if a situation is too neat and orderly, it can feel vitality-depleting. At times like these, you like to stir things up. By amplifying the tension, you feel you can provoke change and unearth matters that were hidden. Before you instinctively ratchet up the temperature, take a moment to consider whether things actually boiling over will cause a mess that will impede your long-term goals.

Your Stellar Self-Care

As the Moon corresponds to our physical body as well as what we find nourishing, the sign of its placement gives us insights into how to best take care of ourselves. Here you'll find nurturing strategies, tips to overcome what causes you stress, and a health focus to pay attention to.

NURTURING STRATEGIES

✳ *Honoring Your Feelings*

You're quite an emotional creature. Your complex feelings guide you and help to illuminate your path, even when you're traveling through more plutonian realms. As such, it's important for you to both explore and honor them. Writing, dancing, listening to music, and doing artwork are some activities that can help you to both channel the wealth of your emotions and better understand them. Consider also working with a trusted guide or therapist to get more emotional clarity. When selecting healthcare practitioners, choose those you feel you can really count on, those who will honor your deeply emotional nature. Find a partner with whom you can share the range of your emotions, including how important it is for you to express your passionate side.

✳ *Testing Your Resolve*

While your all-or-nothing orientation can sometimes stir up stress, in the right situations it can be very motivating, such as inspiring you to dedicate yourself full force to your wellness goals. Your strong resolve, married with your detective skills, can make you relentless when it comes to discovering the causes of and solutions to an array of health challenges. Being magnetized to extremes may also give you the moxie necessary to undertake an activity that may be beneficial although challenging, such as a boot camp workout or deep-tissue massage. And while you usually like to be the one in control, you may find it both powerful and liberating to work with a personal trainer who can push you hard in your pursuit of better fitness.

✳ *The Power of Seduction*

Scorpio is known for its erotic and passionate nature. Connecting to your libidinal urges is vitalizing. In addition to nurturing your sex life, there are other endeavors that can help you rouse and nourish your seductive side. For example, read erotica, research tantra, and practice self-love. Dancing—whether alone or with another—is also a surefire way to stoke the fire within you, notably if it's one that has a sultrier style such as belly dancing, pole dancing, or tango. Another activity to consider is a boudoir session. In this photo shoot, which aims to connect you with the richness of your inner and outer beauty, you are photographed wearing lingerie, sheer clothing, or anything else that has you feel sexy and powerful.

172

STRESS SPOTLIGHT

✳ *Aversion to Superficiality*

You're motivated to probe below the surface to explore riches you know often reside out of sight. This is so essential that when situations don't allow you any space to dig into, you may get irritated. In turn, with a desire to excavate whatever you can, you may probe and prod others, which may cause them to retreat should they feel their buttons being excessively pushed, leaving you feeling isolated. Make sure you're focusing on channeling your efforts to plumb the surface in a conscious way. For example, explore the depth of your subconscious motivations with the help of a trusted therapist. Additionally, learn about spiritual traditions that are steeped in occult knowledge. Or throw yourself into creative projects that will have deeply transformative and healing outcomes. And, if you want support as you're exploring the depths within yourself, all the light and all the shadow, consider Black-Eyed Susan flower essence.

HEALTH FOCUS

✳ *Large Intestines*

Your Moon sign is the one aligned with subjects that are taboo as well as places in which messy, yet transformative, experiences occur. As such, it's not surprising that Scorpio rules the large intestines. Colonic health is essential as it performs numerous instrumental functions, including absorbing water and electrolytes, eliminating waste, and synthesizing nutrients like biotin and vitamin K. Additionally, if we experience bowel irregularity, such as constipation, it can rob us of energy, impede our ability to lose weight, and diminish our sense of overall vitality.

Thankfully, there are numerous lifestyle strategies aimed at maintaining large-intestinal health. As diet is a great place to start, ensure you're eating a bounty of fiber-rich foods such as vegetables, fruits, nuts, seeds, and whole grains. Additionally, fermented foods—such as yogurt, kefir, sauerkraut, and kimchi—contain live active cultures that can help repopulate beneficial intestinal flora, which is a key to good health. Foods such as onions, asparagus, sunchokes, and dandelion greens are packed with fructo-oligosaccharides, a nutrient that helps to support friendly intestinal flora. Some people also opt to supplement with probiotics, notably when traveling or taking antibiotics. As stress can trigger inflammation, activities such as exercise, yoga, and meditation may also benefit colonic health.

Your Sun + Your Moon

Now that you know more about your Moon sign, it's interesting to think about it in relationship with your Sun sign. As these two luminaries are at the foundation of our essential sense of self, looking at your Sun and Moon as a pair can give you additional insights to further understand yourself. Below you will find the twelve pairings associated with the Scorpio Moon.

☀ + ☾		PROFILE
ARIES	SCORPIO	You have strong willpower and a passion to prevail no matter what the challenge. You appreciate movement over stagnancy. Your Aries Sun is lit up charging headfirst into a situation, while your Scorpio Moon feels better when you take a more stealthy approach.
TAURUS	SCORPIO	Your Scorpio Moon adds a deep emotionality to your very practical Taurean nature. You're exceptionally determined; when you set your mind to something, you dig your heels in, clinging to your position with great power. With a strong sensual and erotic side, sexual expression is important to you.
GEMINI	SCORPIO	You like to channel your curiosity into meaningful subjects. Between your Gemini Sun's inquisitiveness and your Scorpio Moon's love to unearth things, you're exceptionally motivated to separate fact from fiction. Honoring your desire to have both breadth and depth of experience is key to your happiness.
CANCER	SCORPIO	People see you as a very sensitive soul who is able to read the waves of hidden currents around them. You're also fiercely protective of your surroundings and those you love. With your emotional Cancer Sun and passionate Scorpio Moon, your feelings are the compass through which you navigate the world.
LEO	SCORPIO	You've got quite a dynamic personality: your Leo Sun loves to shine while your Scorpio Moon gives you a mystique that others find alluring. It's essential that your creative pursuits are infused with meaning. You're passionate about bringing to life works of art that deeply transform people's understanding of themselves.

PROFILE

VIRGO · **SCORPIO**

You prize order but also, at times, have an affinity for disorder. While you place a high price on things being tidy, messiness and disarray sometimes intrigue you. With your analytical Virgo Sun and your probing Scorpio Moon, you've got a fix-it personality that's passionate about problem solving.

LIBRA · **SCORPIO**

Striving for harmony is important to you, but only to a certain extent. After all, while your Libra Sun loves when things are on an even keel, your Scorpio Moon craves the thrill of stormy waters for the emotional stirring that it yields. You're an amazing negotiator whose power derives from both their charm and tenacity.

SCORPIO · **SCORPIO**

As a double Scorpio, you're like the phoenix: when faced with challenges others may find insurmountable, you rise from the ashes, giving birth to a whole new you. Depth and strength are two of your many calling cards. You have a powerful emotional capacity and love to dive below the surface.

SAGITTARIUS · **SCORPIO**

Truth is exceptionally important to you, and you love digging it up while also trying to understand what gives something veracity. With your Sagittarius Sun you crave freedom, while your Scorpio Moon wants to feel intensely connected to others. It's a tricky balance to navigate but you're up for the task.

CAPRICORN · **SCORPIO**

Talk about tenacity: once you set your mind to it, no mountain is too high for you to climb. With your pragmatic Capricorn Sun and your persevering Scorpio Moon, you will pull out all the stops to work hard toward your goals. Feeling empowered and achieving success are very important.

AQUARIUS · **SCORPIO**

You're passionate about social progress. With your intellectual might and emotional chops, you can help communities navigate group dynamics. You have a unique sense of vision: with your Aquarius Sun you've got objectivity, while with your Scorpio Moon you also want to view things up close.

PISCES · **SCORPIO**

You're quite intuitive, able to perceive subtleties that others may not recognize. Within you resides an ocean of emotion, sometimes calm and sometimes turbulent. With your Pisces Sun empathy and your Scorpio Moon passion, you're a dreamer nurtured by understanding the deep ways in which things are connected.

CHAPTER 20

SAGITTARIUS

SYMBOL

The centaur in the act of shooting an arrow, embodying the unbounded freedom of movement and discovery.

ELEMENT

Fire, characterized by the dynamic energy of inspiration, enthusiasm, and passion.

PLANETARY RULER

Jupiter, which represents growth, fortune, faith, and broad understanding.

MODALITY

Mutable, which prizes flexibility, adaptability, and movement.

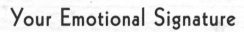

Your Emotional Signature

As the Moon symbolizes instinctive feelings, the sign in which it resides gives us more awareness about the nuances of our emotional nature. Knowing this can help us discern our essential needs, strengthen our superpowers, and be aware of our kryptonite (personal habits that can be challenging).

YOUR ESSENTIAL NEEDS

✳ *Being on the Move*

You love to be in motion. What's satisfying about it isn't just that you're interested in experiencing a new destination. It's also that you are really nurtured by the journey itself, as it provides you with opportunities for learning and adventure. Plus, inertia can feel really stifling as the idea—let alone the experience—of being stagnant can make your energy as well as your mood plunge. Motion is the oxygen that keeps your precious fire from being extinguished. For you, the need for movement isn't confined to the physical realm, but extends to the mental and emotional ones, too. That's why learning is so important, as it shifts your perspective and catalyzes your knowledge base to grow. Similarly, feeling passion for life and having things to look forward to is essential for your emotional well-being. Be like your emblem, the Archer: continue to shoot your arrow and then follow it through the numerous landscapes of your life.

✳ *Being Free*

You cherish freedom, prizing the ability to do what you want when you want. If you feel too confined or limited by obligations, it's likely to make you feel agitated and antsy. And while you know that sometimes you need to, asking for permission isn't your strong suit—you don't want to feel corralled or have others taking liberties with your liberty. With independence so close to your heart, you may also be inspired to work on the behalf of others so that they can feel more emancipated. As wanderlust feeds your soul, you crave having the freedom to explore all that the world offers. This makes you a natural traveler who feels enlivened when there's a journey on the horizon, as well as when you're in the midst of an adventure. When you're free to roam, it gives you a sense of possibility and allows you to discover new things that expand your world.

✳ *Seeking Truth*

You're a truth seeker through and through. Your desire for veracity includes—and definitely extends beyond—wanting to separate fact from fiction. Interested in bigger issues and those fundamental questions that have sparked fascination for scholars throughout history, you're quite philosophical. You naturally gravitate to seeking wisdom as a way to help you answer your favorite questions, those that begin with the word *why*. Given that it's the larger truths that inspire you, you are likely interested in spiritual or religious matters, or you may have eschewed both, if you found that they didn't give you the context necessary to sculpt a sense of meaning. As *truth* is derived from words that mean faith, belief, loyalty, and honesty, it's not surprising that what's also important to you is your personal truth, the code in which you believe, which guides your thoughts and actions.

YOUR SUPERPOWERS

✳ *Enthusiasm*

Your inherent optimism and glass-half-full orientation expand your understanding of what is possible. Married with your enthusiastic nature, when you seize upon something that inspires you, you glisten with buoyant exuberance. You're a natural cheerleader, animated to share your excitement with others, naturally talking up whatever it is that's touched your spirit. Your enthusiasm is so contagious that it often becomes a force that motivates others to learn more about the subject that's gotten you so electrified.

✳ *Joie de Vivre*

You instinctively find joy in life. With your natural desire to live it to its fullest, you seek a wide range of experiences that help you grow and leave you feeling a sense of greater potential. You bring a cheerful attitude of wonder to what you explore and have a knack for spontaneity that arises from your seize-the-day way of orienting. Additionally, your let-the-good-times-roll attitude also allows you to see silver linings that others often don't perceive.

✳ *Vision*

You have a preference to view things through a wide lens, as this enables you to survey the bigger picture, which you seek to understand. Your appreciation for perceiving things in a larger context not only enhances your ability to find inherent meaning in situations, but it's also a skill that draws others to you as they see the benefit it yields. With your eye on the horizon, your sight line aimed at the future, being a visionary comes naturally.

 ## YOUR KRYPTONITE

✳ *Overcommitting*

Brimming with enthusiasm, you get very excited about the potential of various possibilities. And while this can expose you to many adventures, if you sign on too many dotted lines, it can leave you overcommitted. The next thing you know is that you've spread yourself too thin and are not able to give your all to the projects to which you've committed. Remember that saying *no* to some things allows you to say a bigger *yes* to others.

✳ *Dogmatism*

Your beliefs are very important to you. They ground you and help you steer your course through life. Yet, if you are overly attached to your views while also wanting to enthusiastically share them, others could perceive you as proselytizing. This can lead to an outcome opposite to what you intended: instead of turning toward your perspectives, others turn away. To overcome this, as you cherish your viewpoints, be open to alternative perspectives and be aware any time you find yourself nearing a soapbox.

✳ *Pushing Your Limits*

You often push past your limits. In fact, as someone who seeks freedom and embodies great optimism, you sometimes don't even acknowledge that a limit exists. It often takes those moments when you've bitten off more than you can chew to remember that they do. And while overextending yourself brings the thrill of risk, that risk can also result in exhaustion or even reckless injuries. Try to let limits help you know your full potential rather than have you feel limited.

Your Stellar Self-Care

As the Moon corresponds to our physical body as well as what we find nourishing, the sign of its placement gives us insights into how to best take care of ourselves. Here you'll find nurturing strategies, tips to overcome what causes you stress, and a health focus to pay attention to.

NURTURING STRATEGIES

✳ *Having a Goal*

With your Moon in forward-thinking Sagittarius, you love to look ahead into the future, setting your sight on a horizon toward which you journey. Therefore, when it comes to enhancing your well-being, defining your goals can be not only clarifying but also motivating. First consider your larger-scale aims, whether it's meditating daily, sleeping eight hours a night, getting in shape for ski season, or something else. Then, while keeping in mind the date by when you'd like to achieve this goal, create a plan. This includes all the action steps necessary to move you from now to then. At the beginning of each week, write down all the activities you'll do in pursuit of that aim and then every time you do one, check it off and celebrate your progress.

✳ *Cross-cultural Explorations*

Sagittarius is the sign of the traveler, the one who likes to explore the treasures of different lands and cultures. With your Moon here, you've got an orientation that often favors the global over the local. It's easy to channel your interest in being worldly-wise into your self-care regimen. For example, look to the richness of Ayurvedic medicine, which originated in India. There you will find healing practices such as shirodhara and marma therapy and herbs such as ashwagandha, amla, and triphala. Or you can turn to traditional Chinese medicine, with its extensive pharmacopeia of herbal preparations as well as its keystone practices of acupuncture and qigong. You can also indulge your interest in the international by cooking a dish from a different country each week.

✳ *Expanding Your Understanding*

You love learning. Gathering greater awareness speaks to your mind and nourishes your soul. It's not just having knowledge that's important for you but also the process of acquiring it, since it's another way to feel that you're in motion and experiencing growth. In addition to the inclination for information seeking that drives you, you also want to understand the hows and whys that underlie the way things operate. As such, you may be drawn to philosophical, spiritual, and/or psychological orientations as they help you to grasp the bigger picture, something for which you strive. Ensure that you make space in your life for exploration of all kinds, as it will keep you inspired and motivated.

STRESS SPOTLIGHT

✳ *Lack of Motion*

While you need to move, there are times when your mobility may be restricted and you're unable to journey as you desire. You also need to feel moved; and while it's essential for you to feel inspired by life, sometimes mundane responsibilities may seem to be a barrier to having enthralling experiences. A lack of motion doesn't sit well with you and could make you edgy, with an ensuing sense of restlessness causing you stress. Even if you can't travel in the manner you most desire, there's always a way to build in a change of scenery: research your next travel destination, read a book set in a foreign land, listen to a podcast that explores a philosophical topic, and/or take mini-breaks during your workday. If you'd like additional support to guide and inspire you during times of restlessness, consider Angelica flower essence.

HEALTH FOCUS

✳ *Lower Back and Hips*

Governed by Sagittarius, the lower back and hips are important for both stability and mobility. Lower back pain is something that troubles many, and its prevalence increases as we age. While the hips, the largest ball-and-socket joints in the body, are designed to withstand repeated motion, that doesn't preclude them from wear and tear. An assortment of conditions—including osteoporosis, arthritis, and muscle strains—can not only affect the range of motion in the lower back and hips, but also cause pain.

There are many ways we can take care of these parts of our body. To start, ensure that your diet includes enough bone-building nutrients, such as calcium, magnesium, and vitamins D and K. Dietary supplements such as turmeric, glucosamine, and citrus bioflavonoids have anti-inflammatory properties and support cartilage structure. Of course, physical fitness can play a key role: weight-bearing exercise protects against osteoporosis, and Pilates and Gyrotonics can strengthen and stabilize the lower back and hips. Crescent Lunge and Pigeon are two good yoga poses for stretching tight hip flexor muscles. As you may know, one of the biggest culprits of pain and soreness is sitting too much. If you spend lots of time at your workstation, make sure to take frequent breaks and consider getting a standing desk.

Your Sun + Your Moon

Now that you know more about your Moon sign, it's interesting to think about it in relationship with your Sun sign. As these two luminaries are at the foundation of our essential sense of self, looking at your Sun and Moon as a pair can give you additional insights to further understand yourself. Below you will find the twelve pairings associated with the Sagittarius Moon.

☀ + ☾		PROFILE
 ARIES	SAGITTARIUS	Between your fast-moving Aries Sun and your on-the-go Sagittarius Moon, you're up for almost any adventure. What's really important is just being where the action is. You're not one to dwell on the past: for you, it's the present and future where all the action and learning exists.
 TAURUS	SAGITTARIUS	You're both practical and philosophical. You like your creature comforts as well as adventures that take you to unknown territories. With your sensually oriented Taurus Sun and your cosmopolitan Sagittarius Moon, you can find great pleasure in the art, cuisine, and handicrafts of different cultures.
 GEMINI	SAGITTARIUS	With your curious Gemini Sun and your wisdom-seeking Sagittarius Moon, you love collecting facts and then weaving them together to create a broad base of understanding. You have an appreciation for both your immediate environment and the world at large, and you love to think globally and act locally.
CANCER	SAGITTARIUS	Your exploratory Sagittarius Moon propels you to discover the meaning behind family traditions that are so important to your Cancer Sun. It also gives you an expanded view of your emotional responses, enabling you to further understand your feelings. Cooking foods from other cultures may bring you joy.
 LEO	SAGITTARIUS	You're quite a dynamo who has an abundance of creative energy. You love to have fun and find embarking on new discoveries to be really nourishing. With your vibrant Leo Sun and your optimistic Sagittarius Moon, you seek adventures that allow you to radiate the unique person that you are.

PROFILE

 VIRGO	 SAGITTARIUS	With your Virgo Sun, you love the fine details, while with your Sagittarius Moon, the broad picture is what holds allure. Your unique brand of wisdom comes from marrying them both: having reverence for the fine print while understanding the larger context in which it exists.
 LIBRA	 SAGITTARIUS	With your sybaritic Libra Sun and your fun-loving Sagittarius Moon, you're a bon vivant who enjoys the pleasures of life. You love exploring, especially if you can do so with others. You're drawn to relationships with people who broaden your world and infuse you with optimism.
 SCORPIO	 SAGITTARIUS	It's essential that you feel you're in movement, whether that's physically or emotionally. It's important for you to balance your desire for deep connection with your need to feel free. Between your probing Scorpio Sun and your inquisitive Sagittarius Moon, getting to the truth of the matter is essential.
 SAGITTARIUS	 SAGITTARIUS	As a double Sagittarius, making meaning of your life is really important. You're quite connected to your ever-evolving principles, which serve as a compass to help you navigate the landscape of life. Having the freedom to move about and explore new territories is essential to your happiness.
 CAPRICORN	 SAGITTARIUS	You've got both a hardworking and visionary nature. You can readily set future goals and then figure out what needs to get done to accomplish them. Your optimistic Sagittarius Moon helps your pragmatic Capricorn Sun to look at things from a glass-half-full perspective more frequently.
 AQUARIUS	 SAGITTARIUS	Talk about a mover and shaker who prizes their freedom and has their eyes on the future. As you look ahead, you're always envisioning how to make the world a better place. Your passionate Sagittarius Moon lends your rational Aquarius Sun a dose of get-up-and-go motivation to move your ideas forward.
PISCES	SAGITTARIUS	You're a philosopher and a mystic who loves to explore spiritual topics on your quest to find the meaning of life. Doing so brings more enrichment to yourself and others. Your active Sagittarius Moon gives your pacific Pisces Sun the spark of energy necessary to take the actions required to make your dreams come true.

CHAPTER 21

CAPRICORN

SYMBOL

The Sea Goat, known for its persistence, sure-footedness, and committed guardianship of its resources.

ELEMENT

Earth, characterized by the grounded energy of creativity, resilience, and practicality.

PLANETARY RULER

Saturn, which represents time, rules, and responsibilities, elemental to turning ideas into reality.

MODALITY

Cardinal, which prizes initiation, ambition, and being enterprising.

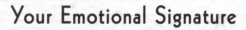

Your Emotional Signature

As the Moon symbolizes instinctive feelings, the sign in which it resides gives us more awareness about the nuances of our emotional nature. Knowing this can help us discern our essential needs, strengthen our superpowers, and be aware of our kryptonite (personal habits that can be challenging).

YOUR ESSENTIAL NEEDS

✳ *Accomplishing Things*

You've got a job to do—or many, actually—and you couldn't be happier. You love teeing up your to-do list, anticipating the satisfaction you'll receive later when you check things off. It's exciting to think how when you invest your resources, including time and effort, you get a practical payoff, something that you know you had a direct hand in bringing to life. Achieving things makes you proud and gives you more confidence to continue in your pursuits. It also brings you success and recognition, both of which are so meaningful to you. Plus, the more that you achieve and cement your track record, the more you feel like an authority. You like to climb things, whether career ladders or proverbial mountains. And while getting to the top may be your goal, you also find the ascent—in which you experience your amazing industrious capacity—to be quite rewarding.

✳ *Leaving a Legacy*

As noted, achievements are very important to you. They are an emblem of your hard work, the bricks on your road to success. And when you get recognition for your accomplishments, it feels really good to you. What's essential, though, is not just how people think of you now but also how they will in the future. As such, you look to your legacy with great regard. It's so meaningful that it's a regular factor in guiding your decision making, as you often think about what you want to leave behind after you're gone. This informs the paths you elect to pursue and the commitments you make. There are many ways to leave a legacy: through your career or raising a family, through a creative project or contribution to your community, or all of the above. Regardless of the ones you pursue, you find leaving your mark on the world to be really motivating and quite satisfying.

✳ *Being Responsible*

From a young age, you forged a sense of duty. Those with a Capricorn Moon often grow up fast, finding that they needed to take care of themselves and others in ways usually left for those much older. In turn, this ends up informing much of your orientation to life: it makes you quite self-sufficient and molds you into a beacon of responsibility. It's important to you to be a reliable parent (or aunt or uncle), unwavering team player, and fearless breadwinner. Your reputation for dependability often precedes you. People rely upon you for assistance of all kinds, and they trust that you're concerned as well as steadfast in your commitments. As you mentor them, it also gives you an opportunity to emphasize the virtue of due diligence and hard work. All that said, it's important to remember that while you may feel obligated to help others, your first responsibility should always be to yourself.

YOUR SUPERPOWERS

✳ *Allegiance*

You cherish commitments. When you give your word, it's as good as gold. While it takes time for you to trust people enough to invite them into your inner circle, once you do, they can be assured of your allegiance and that they can count on you to go the extra mile for them. They need to know this, though: you will be devoted as long as they are. If you sense that they are not upholding their loyal commitment, you won't either.

✳ *Persistence*

You don't give up. No matter how long something may take, once you commit, you resolve to get the job done. Part of the reason that you have the capacity to see things through is because of your wellspring of endurance. What contributes to this staying power is your slow and steady pace: you may not be quick out of the gate, but all bets are on you to finish the marathon, not only with grace but also in top place.

✳ *Industriousness*

It doesn't bother you to work hard; you're accustomed to it and find it enjoyable. Your time is occupied with duties, projects, and things to construct, to which you attend with diligence, responsibility, and the wisdom earned from lots of past experience. Witnessing the fruits of your labor really motivates you. Your tireless efforts and ability to get so much done have won you the accolades of colleagues, who often wonder whether somehow you magically have access to more than twenty-four hours each day.

YOUR KRYPTONITE

✳ *Overwork*

You are really hardworking: it's not just because you feel obligated to be, but that you also really like getting things done. Yet, with all the time you dedicate to laboring, it doesn't leave much space for relaxing. This can stress your relationships, not to mention your mind and body. Remember that relaxation and responsibility aren't mutually exclusive. In fact, taking the time to unwind will reduce your stress so you'll be able to work with more ease and concentration.

✳ *Frugality*

Being thoughtful about spending money or sharing resources is not a bad thing. What can cause stress, though, is when you're overly conservative when you need not be. As you've likely experienced, saying *no* when it's not really necessary can make your life feel rather restrictive. Not sure if your penny wise is also pound foolish? Tune in to see whether it's derived from the reality of your current situation or being sourced from feeling a sense of scarcity that sometimes shadows you.

✳ *Solemnity*

You're a serious person. It's not that you can't do humor—you're the master of sarcasm, after all. It's just that with your sense of responsibility and commitment to achievement, you often take a no-nonsense approach to everything. Unfortunately, your somber outlook could leave you dispirited at times. Remember that while life can be hard, it can also be beautiful, and that sometimes it's possible to be earnest while also looking at things through the lens of levity.

Your Stellar Self-Care

As the Moon corresponds to our physical body as well as what we find nourishing, the sign of its placement gives us insights into how to best take care of ourselves. Here you'll find nurturing strategies, tips to overcome what causes you stress, and a health focus to pay attention to.

NURTURING STRATEGIES

✳ *Taking a Conservative Approach*

Keeping well doesn't have to create a deep well in your wallet. In fact, some of the best things in life are free or low cost. There are many online classes you can take that will help you break a sweat without breaking your budget. Or go even more low tech: taking regular walks wearing a weighted backpack will help you build bone while burning extra calories. Meditation is one of the best things to do for holistic well-being, and it's completely free. Additionally, research your insurance plan to see whether it offers benefits for massage, chiropractic, and/or acupuncture services. Growing oregano, rosemary, and/or thyme on your windowsill is an inexpensive way to enjoy these nutrient-rich herbs and forge a deeper connection to the natural world.

✳ *Architecting a Plan*

As Capricorn is the master architect, designing and following blueprints is really satisfying to those with this Moon sign. Use this to your benefit when it comes to your well-being by envisioning a new structure that you want to create: perhaps it's learning to cook healthy meals, exercising five days a week, getting eight hours of sleep, or some other wellness goal. First, survey and then declare why achieving it is so instrumental to your well-being. Then envision how you will feel once your aim has been realized. From there, consider the activities needed to achieve your goals, sketching out a schedule of what they are and when you will implement them. Be confident that as you take these steps, you are laying down the bricks of a new approach that will pave the way for greater well-being.

✳ *Moisturizing and Hydrating*

Given that both the skin and the quality of dryness are associated with Capricorn, it's important to keep your skin hydrated so it can look and feel its best. A starting strategy: drink adequate amounts of water daily. While an essential wellness activity, it may not be your strong suit since hardworking Capricorn Moons often perceive it as a diversion from attending to the many tasks they have at hand. Ensure that your diet is providing you with adequate omega-3 fatty acids (found in cold-water fish, walnuts, purslane, and chia and hemp seeds) as well as deeply colored antioxidant-rich fruits and vegetables. Exfoliate your skin regularly using a gentle scrub or glycolic acid toner. Additionally, use a high-quality moisturizer; if you have sensitive skin, test several to ensure that they don't contain allergens that will provoke a reaction.

STRESS SPOTLIGHT

✳ *Burnout*

You set out to accomplish great things. To marshal the sense of security you crave, you work tirelessly towards your aims, with success often being the only goal that matters. And while you may achieve a multitude of feats, the path is often peppered with stress and tension; after all, with your eye always on the prize, you're likely to abdicate time for fun and relaxation. As you've likely experienced, working so hard can lead to burnout and the exhaustion, disrupted sleep, and frustration that it yields. As a hard worker, try to also work hard on making space for enjoyment. And remember that asking for help to get things done is a sign of strength, not weakness. If you're looking for a flower essence that can help you to reduce the unrelenting demands you place on yourself, consider Oak.

HEALTH FOCUS

✳ *Joints*

Capricorn is the sign associated with the joints, the parts of the body where bones meet. Some joints are rigid—such as those in the skull—while others are moveable. The latter includes the shoulders, hips, and knees. They play a critical role in not only maintaining structural integrity but our ability to effortlessly move. With their complex architecture, joints are delicate and can be the site of sprains or inflammation, which can cause pain and limit mobility.

Ensuring your diet features adequate amounts of foods rich in anti-inflammatory nutrients is key to joint health. These include cold-water fish, walnuts, purslane, and chia and hemp seeds (rich in omega-3s) and deeply colored fruits and vegetables (concentrated in carotenoid and flavonoid nutrients). Spices such as ginger and turmeric also have notably anti-inflammatory properties. Furthermore, regular exercise is important as it keeps your joints lubricated, strengthens surrounding muscles, and enhances bone density. If you're especially concerned about your knees, shedding excess weight can be beneficial. Practicing good posture—when standing and sitting as well as lifting and carrying things—is also essential for joint care. Craniosacral therapy is a gentle treatment that many find relaxing: the practitioner cradles and rocks your head as they work to lightly adjust the cranial bones and enhance the flow of cerebrospinal fluid.

Your Sun + Your Moon

Now that you know more about your Moon sign, it's interesting to think about it in relationship with your Sun sign. As these two luminaries at are the foundation of our essential sense of self, looking at your Sun and Moon as a pair can give you additional insights to further understand yourself. Below you will find the twelve pairings associated with the Capricorn Moon.

☀ + ☾		PROFILE
ARIES	**CAPRICORN**	You love to champion causes and work hard to achieve your aims. You can pull strength from both your Aries Sun's fast-moving instinctive nature and your Capricorn Moon's ability to proceed slowly. Balancing your risk-taking and conservative sides is key to your success.
TAURUS	**CAPRICORN**	You're exceptionally pragmatic, with a fond appreciation for the natural world and working hard to achieve the success you treasure. Your Capricorn Moon gives you the tried-and-true know-how to create routines that will honor your Taurus Sun's love of experiencing sensual pleasure.
GEMINI	**CAPRICORN**	Your Gemini Sun instills you with a love of learning; your Capricorn Moon gives you the persistence to bring your goals to fruition. You have both light-on-your-feet versatility and grounded-on-the earth pragmatism. Giving space to your desire for variety and need to be single-focused is key to finding balance.
CANCER	**CAPRICORN**	Your appreciation for tradition and reverence for the past guide how you approach life. With your Cancer Sun, you're quite emotional, and with your Capricorn Moon, you've also got a strong pragmatic side. You don't shy away from doing the work that can help you nourish your emotional life.
LEO	**CAPRICORN**	You're a creative who has the moxie to bring your artistic visions to life. Between your Leo Sun's love of encouraging others and your Capricorn Moon's attraction to getting things done, you have great leadership skills. At times you can be generous while at others frugal. Finding ways to honor both is important.

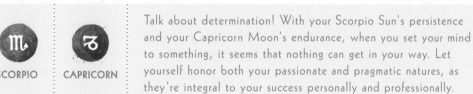
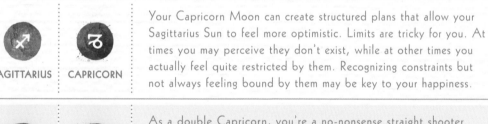
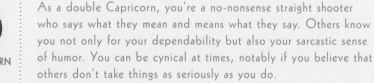
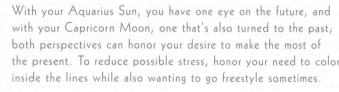
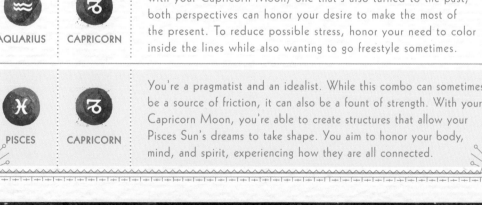

☀ + ☾

PROFILE

VIRGO · **CAPRICORN**

You're a master at the practical. Your innate knowledge of navigating the system allows you to be of service, something inherently important to you. Between your organization-oriented Virgo Sun and your hardworking Capricorn Moon, architecting sustainable solutions is both a skill and key to your success.

LIBRA · **CAPRICORN**

With your Libra Sun, relationships are important to you. And with your loyalty-honoring Capricorn Moon, you often draw a decisive line between those in your inner and outer circles. You're happy to have numerous social connections; it's those who have shown long-term dependability to whom you have true allegiance.

SCORPIO · **CAPRICORN**

Talk about determination! With your Scorpio Sun's persistence and your Capricorn Moon's endurance, when you set your mind to something, it seems that nothing can get in your way. Let yourself honor both your passionate and pragmatic natures, as they're integral to your success personally and professionally.

SAGITTARIUS · **CAPRICORN**

Your Capricorn Moon can create structured plans that allow your Sagittarius Sun to feel more optimistic. Limits are tricky for you. At times you may perceive they don't exist, while at other times you actually feel quite restricted by them. Recognizing constraints but not always feeling bound by them may be key to your happiness.

CAPRICORN · **CAPRICORN**

As a double Capricorn, you're a no-nonsense straight shooter who says what they mean and means what they say. Others know you not only for your dependability but also your sarcastic sense of humor. You can be cynical at times, notably if you believe that others don't take things as seriously as you do.

AQUARIUS · **CAPRICORN**

With your Aquarius Sun, you have one eye on the future, and with your Capricorn Moon, one that's also turned to the past; both perspectives can honor your desire to make the most of the present. To reduce possible stress, honor your need to color inside the lines while also wanting to go freestyle sometimes.

PISCES · **CAPRICORN**

You're a pragmatist and an idealist. While this combo can sometimes be a source of friction, it can also be a fount of strength. With your Capricorn Moon, you're able to create structures that allow your Pisces Sun's dreams to take shape. You aim to honor your body, mind, and spirit, experiencing how they are all connected.

CHAPTER 22

AQUARIUS

SYMBOL

The Water Bearer, who gathers wisdom and insight, offering it in service to humanity.

ELEMENT

Air, characterized by the agile energy of observation, logic, and sociability.

PLANETARY RULERS

Saturn, which represents time, rules, and responsibilities, elemental to turning ideas into reality; and Uranus, which inspires innovation, sudden revelations, rebellion, and creative chaos.

MODALITY

Fixed, which prizes reliability, predictability, and stamina.

Your Emotional Signature

As the Moon symbolizes instinctive feelings, the sign in which it resides gives us more awareness about the nuances of our emotional nature. Knowing this can help us discern our essential needs, strengthen our superpowers, and be aware of our kryptonite (personal habits that can be challenging).

YOUR ESSENTIAL NEEDS

✱ *Partaking in Community*

You thrive when aligned with a group, and love coming together with others who share your visions and values. You inherently know that there is power in numbers, essential for pursuing the causes you find to have utmost importance. Being in a group lets you experience the value of contributing to something larger than yourself. And you can do so from a spot that keeps you in your comfort zone: standing back and approaching situations with distance and objectivity, rather than having to get up close and personal with too many people. With your appreciation for the power of networks, and knowledge that evolution involves a multiplicity of dynamic factors, groups also capture your attention because they are like a microcosm of other systems at work. Additionally, being a part of a collective not only gives you a sense of belonging, but it allows you to further understand the nuances of humanity, which you find endlessly fascinating.

✱ *Having Space*

With a strong need for freedom, you don't like to be hemmed in, whether by people, schedule constraints, or select societal conventions. You need space to be your unique self, the latitude to march to the beat of your own drum, and the independence to take the road less traveled (a pathway you adore). The space in which you spend time, and the time in which you are in certain spaces, is also important. As you're so sensitive to energies, if it doesn't have a certain flow, it may impede your bright mind's ability to efficiently process the multitude of inputs to which you usually have access. You have an appreciation for emptiness, the area that connects two points, as you understand the creative power it may hold. Reflecting its unbound and intricately woven-together nature, the subject of outer space—and the stars and planets contained within it—inspires and captivates you.

✱ *Helping the World*

You have a future-forward orientation, concerned not only about the now but moments yet to occur. Between this and your altruistic spirit, you have a passion for co-creating change that will inspire progress and make the world a better place. You're able to tap into an almost selfless concern for the well-being of others, interested in creating systems that can spark beneficial change for individuals and groups of people. The ins and outs of societal structures fascinate you, and you have a sharp eye for not only their failings but ways to spearhead beneficial advancements. The route you take to create betterment may be radical in both senses of the word: it's not only innovative and may reflect a departure from traditions, but seeks to reform things by working on the roots rather than the glossy factors that reside on the surface.

YOUR SUPERPOWERS

✳ Pattern Recognition

You've got a bright mind that has a 360-degree way of viewing things, able to see situations via numerous vantage points, sometimes all at once. This gives you a masterful ability to recognize patterns, something you find quite enthralling. You have laser-like vision that helps you perceive how an orchestra of elements is arranged. You're blessed with the innate ability to effortlessly zoom in and out, so that you can see how everything is connected, whether through their similarities or differences.

✳ Originality

You've got a flair for innovation. Often seen as a vanguard, others are inspired not only by your original style, but also your ability to readily perceive state-of-the-art solutions. Your proximity to the cutting edge is sourced from various factors: you've got an eye on the future, eschew confines of the traditional, and have highly attuned perceptive skills. You've got more courage than most to be different, which helps you to embody your individuality.

✳ Altruism

What's so special about you is not just that you care about the world at large; it's that you marry an interest in helping to make the world a better place with the intellectual chops to create a plan and envision ways to put it into action. With your bright mind and progressive vision, you're able to channel your humanitarian concerns into collective activities that allow you to join together with others to do a vast amount of good.

YOUR KRYPTONITE

✳ *Intellectualization*

No one would contest that you have strong mental prowess; it's just that sometimes your head takes over and crowds out your heart. When this happens, you may become hyper-focused on whether things make sense at the expense of how they make you or others feel. Additionally, it can have you spending a lot of time in your mind rather than paying attention to your physical well-being. Honor your powerful thoughts while tuning into your body and emotions.

✳ *Detachment*

At times, you like to keep your distance. It gives you the space to avoid obligations that may weigh you down, disabling your ability to work on your passion projects. Unfortunately, though, at times this may lead to people wondering whether you're interested in them; in turn, they may distance themselves from you, leaving you feeling isolated. Even if you only spend limited time with people, being really present with them will foster the free-flow sharing of ideas, something you cherish.

✳ *Rebellion*

You have a hard time when you perceive your freedom to be your quirky self and express your future-forward ideas is being constrained. You have limited patience for "shoulds" and hate feeling bound by social conventions that don't leave any room for individuality. When you face either, you may find your inner revolutionary gets activated. While there's nothing wrong with being a freedom fighter, just watch that it has intention behind it and that you're a rebel with a cause, rather than without one.

Your Stellar Self-Care

As the Moon corresponds to our physical body as well as what we find nourishing, the sign of its placement gives us insights into how to best take care of ourselves. Here you'll find nurturing strategies, tips to overcome what causes you stress, and a health focus to pay attention to.

NURTURING STRATEGIES

✳ *Alternative Approaches*

You're an open-minded trailblazer who likes to chart their own course. This usually has you adopting non-mainstream approaches before others. For example, you were likely using acupuncture, aromatherapy, and dietary supplements much earlier than your friends. Continuing to seek out cutting-edge therapies and self-care activities may be satisfying for you. For example, researching and trying treatments considered peripheral—for example, sound therapy, bio-energetic testing, forest bathing, lucid dreaming, crystal healing, or others—may help you discover exciting and novel wellness solutions. That's not to say that you should forgo modern medicine and the advantages it carries, but as a person with a great ability to weave together unique tapestries, you can integrate both alternative and allopathic approaches into a holistic web for wellness.

✳ *Energetic Medicine*

Your Moon sign is the one associated with electricity, circuitry, and subtle life force energy. Therefore, enjoying healing practices that work on an energetic level may be right up your alley. While there are many therapies and activities under the umbrella of energetic medicine, one example is reiki. In this hands-on healing therapy, practitioners, while thinking of different sacred symbols, direct energy to help inspire a person's innate healing abilities. Another is homeopathy, which features remedies made from very dilute forms of natural substances that operate on a subtle energy level to try to bring about a restoration of health. Additionally, qigong and tai chi are meditative movement practices that facilitate your awareness of the vibrational fields within and around you.

✳ *Group Healing*

As shared before, those with Aquarius Moons love connecting with other people. As being involved with groups can be nourishing, it may be a strategy to honor in your wellness regimen. For example, see whether exercising in a group setting, even if via an online class, is more motivating than doing it solo. And, if you want to get some counseling but doing it one-on-one doesn't meet your needs, consider group therapy. Another method done in workshop is Systemic Family Constellations, which brings about greater awareness and healing through uncovering multigenerational family dynamics. Groups can provide amazing support. We only need to look at the success of programs that help those struggling with alcohol, gambling, and other addictions to recognize the power of fellowship.

STRESS SPOTLIGHT

✳ *Fitting In*

Belonging is a key theme for those with an Aquarius Moon, and sometimes you may struggle with feeling like you belong and fit in. After all, between your nonconformist nature and your perceptive mind, you sometimes wonder whether you mesh well with people. As much as you're an individualist, this can cause you upset and worry. Remember that, just as you want to maintain your individuality and march to the beat of your own drum, so do many others. Have faith that you can find people and collectives that share your vision and values so that you don't need to compromise who you are to experience a sense of belonging. If you need support perceiving how you fit in to a community matrix, allowing you to feel even more connected, consider Quaking Grass flower essence.

HEALTH FOCUS

✳ *Circulatory System*

As a sign that governs networks, it's not surprising that Aquarius rules the circulatory system, along with the arteries, veins, and capillaries that compose it. This web of vessels transports blood—and the oxygen, nutrients, and hormones it contains—throughout our body. As you know, maintaining the health of your circulatory system is key for well-being. Circulatory system problems can cause muscle cramps and cold feet, as well as conditions such as hypertension, heart disease, and varicose veins.

There are a host of nutrients known for enhancing the function of the circulatory system. These include omega-3 fatty acids and vitamins C and E. Also beneficial for bolstering blood vessels are the flavonoid phytonutrients found in purple- and red-colored fruits and vegetables, dark chocolate, and green tea. Exercise, of course, is important for maintaining circulatory health as it increases blood flow. There are also some self-care treatments thought to benefit the peripheral circulatory system, used by many who are prone to varicose veins. These include going on regular walks, taking vein-strengthening herbs (such as butcher's broom, horse chestnut, and gotu kola), and applying witch hazel compresses. Just note: if you have leg circulation issues, before practicing self-care, check in with a doctor who can rule out that you don't have a more serious condition known as chronic venous insufficiency.

Your Sun + Your Moon

Now that you know more about your Moon sign, it's interesting to think about it in relationship with your Sun sign. As these two luminaries are at the foundation of our essential sense of self, looking at your Sun and Moon as a pair can give you additional insights to further understand yourself. Below you will find the twelve pairings associated with the Aquarius Moon.

☀ + ☾		PROFILE
ARIES	**AQUARIUS**	You're quite the pioneer. With an Aries Sun, you're a self-starter, while with an Aquarius Moon, you're nourished by innovation and experimentation. At once instinctive and cerebral, you like to be involved with numerous communities and collectives. You're a champion inspired by both your passion and reasoning.
TAURUS	**AQUARIUS**	You approach matters slowly. As long as you know that there's an exit door should you require it, you have a lot of staying power. You're able to bring your Taurus practical know-how to the technology- and group-oriented projects so enjoyed by your Aquarius Moon.
GEMINI	**AQUARIUS**	You love to learn: it helps you make sense of things both for yourself and others. Like the wind, you need freedom to be on the move, to dash here and there. Between your curious Gemini Sun and your philanthropic Aquarius Moon, you like investigating ways to help people live a better life.
CANCER	**AQUARIUS**	You've got one eye on the past and one on the future; when you honor these different vantage points, your present can really come to life. With a family-oriented Cancer Sun and a freedom-honoring Aquarius Moon, you strive to take care of those you love while also honoring everyone's need to have a bit of space.
LEO	**AQUARIUS**	Working on community-oriented creative projects is really nourishing as you get to express your unique Leo self while helping others—inherently important to an Aquarius Moon. Recognition can be tricky, as sometimes you want applause for your efforts while at other moments you'd rather slip into the crowd and go unnoticed.

VIRGO	**AQUARIUS**	You're keen to understand patterns, notably if doing so makes you more efficient. Aiming your fix-it Virgo nature at the social issues in which your Aquarius Moon is interested can be really satisfying. Your high ideals can help you craft solutions for good; just keep tabs that they don't have you being overly critical.
LIBRA	**AQUARIUS**	You treasure relationships. Whether it's hanging out with your partner or spending the evening with a flock of friends, being social brings you pleasure. While with a Libra Sun you are sometimes indecisive, your Aquarius Moon gives you the ability to survey the landscape, which can expedite decision-making.
SCORPIO	**AQUARIUS**	Your Scorpio Sun is passionate about being up close and personal while your Aquarius Moon loves to keep its distance; the ability to balance these qualities is key. Gathering with others who are interested in exploring the mysteries of life and researching solutions not readily apparent on the surface can be very satisfying activities.
SAGITTARIUS	**AQUARIUS**	You need to be free to explore, navigating through an expanse of different landscapes, ideas, and/or groups of people. With a Sagittarius Sun, you love to travel, while with your Aquarius Moon, you're a citizen of the world; discovering the riches of other cultures can bring you great fulfillment.
CAPRICORN	**AQUARIUS**	You cherish the ordinary and the extra-ordinary, honoring both the lessons you attained in the past while also keen to learn from upcoming experiences. With a Capricorn Sun, you prize tradition, while your Aquarius Moon gets electrified by innovative solutions. Making space for both brings you strength and power.
AQUARIUS	**AQUARIUS**	As a double Aquarius, you've got a Promethean spirit, bent on helping others in your own unique way. With your bright mind, you're able to get glimpses of insight as if out of nowhere. These *aha!* moments both inspire you and serve as a beacon to guide you.
PISCES	**AQUARIUS**	You're a romantic on a mission. Having space gives you clarity, allowing you to both dream and have the distance necessary to be objective. Between your sensitive Pisces Sun and your humanitarian Aquarius Moon, you're an idealist who wants to help people and make the world a better place.

CHAPTER 23

PISCES

SYMBOL

A pair of Fish, bound together yet swimming in opposite directions, symbolizing the integration of the spiritual and material worlds.

ELEMENT

Water, characterized by fluidity, emotionality, reflection, and nonlinear understanding.

MODALITY

Mutable, which prizes flexibility, adaptability, and movement.

PLANETARY RULERS

Jupiter, which represents growth, fortune, faith, and broad understanding; and Neptune, which inspires unity, transcendence, and a connection to the numinous.

Your Emotional Signature

As the Moon symbolizes instinctive feelings, the sign in which it resides gives us more awareness about the nuances of our emotional nature. Knowing this can help us discern our essential needs, strengthen our superpowers, and be aware of our kryptonite (personal habits that can be challenging).

YOUR ESSENTIAL NEEDS

✳ *Letting Yourself Dream*

Sometimes the walkabout world feels uninspiring to someone with a Pisces Moon. You long for a world infused with technicolor vibrancy, steeped in beauty, kindness, and love. Unfortunately, reality sometimes doesn't meet your ideal. And yet, with your vivid imaginative capacities and ability to seemingly travel to different worlds, you can tap into a sea of inspirations that nurture your heart and soul. As you allow your mind to drift, you may perceive nuanced insights that inform you as to how you want to live your life. Your dreams can also be your portal to the muse, galvanizing ideas that you can channel into artistic and creative activities, as well as things you want to manifest in your life. And while your nighttime oneiric visions may bring awareness, make sure to also create space for your mind to wander during the day.

✳ *Radiating Love*

You swim in vast oceans of emotions, and tenderness and caring are some of your favorite waves to surf. As you have a talent for understanding the innate goodness that resides in everyone, you're able to tap into an almost superhuman capacity to forgive. This contributes to your ability to shower others with love. It's important to have many vessels into which you can pour your care and compassion. If not, it may create too much pressure on your primary relationships, notably if they can't hold and mirror back your kindness and unwavering allegiance. For example, channeling your love into your professional and community work can have you find outlets in which you can make a difference in the lives of many. Streaming it into artistic projects not only allows you to tap more deeply into its wellspring but can have you forge creations that move, touch, and inspire others.

✳ *Connecting to the Magic*

You're magnetized to experience the magic you perceive inherent in this world, drawn to events that leave you feeling buoyant and effervescent. As you find glamour really captivating, whether it's enjoying fancy cocktails at a five-star hotel or losing yourself in a stack of fashion magazines, you're charmed by experiences that seem to transcend mundane reality. You instinctively view life through a poetic and symbolic lens, often perceiving subtleties and nuances that make it more enchanting. You are hyperaware of how things can be both separate and interwoven. As such, you cherish experiencing synchronicity: situations of acausal coincidence in which an external event mirrors the thoughts and feelings currently arising in your internal world. When you encounter synchronicity, it may leave you in awe. You remember that there is some sort of invisible web that connects us all, which is a concept you find really comforting.

YOUR SUPERPOWERS

✳ *Imagination*

Your imagination is one of your great gifts, allowing you to access a plethora of insights and ideas cordoned off from your rational mind. Being so imaginative lends itself to the artistic expression you cherish while also helping you dream up new inventions. Books, movies, and music not only inspire your imagination, but allow you to be readily transported to different worlds from which you access a myriad of feelings and inspirations.

✳ *Compassion*

You see yourself in others and others in yourself. Your natural ability to stand in another's shoes gives rise to the empathetic way that you interact with people. You love experiencing deep connection and understanding how someone is feeling. With your compassionate nature, you don't want to just relate with them, you want to help. You're motivated to perform random acts of kindness that you perceive will benefit others, whether by inspiring them with joy or relieving them of suffering.

✳ *Clair Senses*

You're quite intuitive, with the ability to directly perceive insights in a way that often bypasses reasoning. This allows you to tap into an ocean of awareness that helps you navigate your life as well as guide others. Your strong sixth sense provides you with great clarity and may arise in one or several ways: through vision (clairvoyance), sound (clairaudience), feeling (clairsentience), smell (clairalience), or taste (clairgustance). Tune in to which of these are your strong suits and work to further develop your perceptive skills.

YOUR KRYPTONITE

✳ *Escapism*

As someone with such a vivid imagination, you often retreat to reverie, notably when life leaves you disappointed and disillusioned. With your exceptional sensitivity, you're often flooded with feelings. As a result, you may seek substances, activities, or behaviors that help you either tune out or make things seem infused with additional inspiration. If you find yourself being an escape artist, try to get away through more uplifting channels, like spiritual or creative pursuits.

✳ *Sacrifice*

You're so sensitive that when others suffer, so do you. As an empath, you feel so compelled to help, which can lead to giving away your resources—whether time, energy, money, or other precious objects. After a while, notably if there's no reciprocity, you may feel depleted and upset, even taking on the role of the victim or martyr. Remember that while you can't help being so caring, sometimes saying *no* can be as compassionate (if not more so) than saying *yes*.

✳ *Avoidance*

Things may often be overwhelming to someone so sensitive, with even the most mundane tasks sometimes spurring an orchestra of feelings—worry, regret, or fear—that can stop you in your tracks. You may even see them as boring, a diversion from the flowing, dreamy space you prefer to inhabit. From there, you may proceed to one of your go-to strategies: avoidance. Since out of sight rarely translates to out of mind, do what you can to not turn a blind eye to those things that require visibility.

Your Stellar Self-Care

As the Moon corresponds to our physical body as well as what we find nourishing, the sign of its placement gives us insights into how to best take care of ourselves. Here you'll find nurturing strategies, tips to overcome what causes you stress, and a health focus to pay attention to.

NURTURING STRATEGIES

✳ *Be in the Flow*

Those with the Moon in Pisces are nurtured when they feel unconstrained and can connect to a sense of flow. Give yourself space during a given day and don't schedule any activities—just see what you are inspired to do at that moment. Feel a sense of flow in your body by freestyle dancing; turn on your favorite tunes and just see how your body wants to move. Using markers, pastels, or a pencil, spend some time doodling. Instead of setting out with an intention of what you want to draw, be a mindful witness to what designs you create. You can also connect to a sense of flow through floating. Whether it's taking a bath, going for a swim, or using a flotation device, the buoyancy of the water can be really supportive for your fluid nature.

✳ *Opening to Your Dreams*

You're a dreamer who's tapped into your dreams, both your aspirations for how you imagine life should unfold as well as your nightly oneiric visions. Regarding the latter, your dreams can be a powerful portal to the inherent wisdom you carry. And as a person who appreciates symbology and nonlinear narratives, turning to your dreams can nurture your body, mind, and spirit. An essential step in creating a dreamwork practice is to keep a dream journal. This has numerous benefits, including that regularly recording dreams may help to enhance your ability to recall them. Plus, if they are documented in one spot, you can readily review and decode them, as well as see the connections between numerous ones.

✳ *Prayerful Rituals*

Those with a Pisces Moon have an air of soulfulness to them. They are nourished by the belief that they are connected to something greater than themselves. Add to that your view that thoughts and intention-infused actions have power, and you can see why devotional practices may be nurturing. Research has suggested that a regular prayer practice—whether done alone or with others—has beneficial effects on emotional well-being, including reducing symptoms of depression and anxiety. Another way to invite sanctity into your life is to say a blessing before enjoying a meal. You could also create an altar in which you place sacred objects and visit it each day.

 ## STRESS SPOTLIGHT

✳ *Boundary Issues*

Boundaries are tricky for those with Pisces Moons. After all, as you sense that everything is inherently connected, where you begin and another ends can be unclear. Add to this that you're a psychic sponge, able to readily sense the subtle energies eddying around you, and it's easy to understand how you may often be flooded with feelings of disquietude. The solution is not to be rigid and uncaring, as that's seemingly impossible anyway. Rather, know that you can still exude compassion while also setting personal limits. In fact, doing so will give you the clarity and vitality necessary to channel your giving spirit more consciously. Energetic hygiene practices—such as taking an Epsom salt bath and doing aura-clearing exercises—can also be helpful. If you're looking for a flower essence that can help you strengthen your emotional boundaries, consider Pink Yarrow.

205

 ## HEALTH FOCUS

✳ *Feet*

At first blush, it may seem surprising that the feet, our connection point to the earth, are governed by Pisces, more known for its head-in-the-clouds disposition. It's actually quite perfect that the soles are connected to your soulful sign, since staying grounded is so important for manifesting the dreams and visions that are essential to you.

Wearing shoes with good arch support and not overdoing it with stilettos is key for avoiding conditions such as blisters, plantar fasciitis, and bunions. Regular pedicures aren't just a treat for the feet, but can also have therapeutic value, staving off ingrown toenails and softening calluses. If you're looking to heal cracked heels, add some myrrh essential oil to unscented lotion and massage your feet with it. Plagued with pesky athlete's foot? Wash your feet daily with mild soap, making sure to dry them well, including in the areas between your toes; apply antifungal tea tree oil—mixed with some unscented massage oil—to the affected areas. Reflexology treatment, a massage in which the practitioner applies pressure to areas of the foot corresponding to different body parts, is not just relaxing but can give your overall well-being a boost.

Your Sun + Your Moon

Now that you know more about your Moon sign, it's interesting to think about it in relationship with your Sun sign. As these two luminaries are at the foundation of our essential sense of self, looking at your Sun and Moon as a pair can give you additional insights to further understand yourself. Below you will find the twelve pairings associated with the Pisces Moon.

☀ + ☾		PROFILE
ARIES	**PISCES**	You're a champion with a heart of gold. When you let your inspirational musings guide your movements, your dreams can more readily become a reality. With your Aries Sun, sometimes you like to spearhead actions, while with your Pisces Moon, at other moments you're quite satisfied to go with the flow.
TAURUS	**PISCES**	With your Taurus Sun, you love navigating through your five senses, and with your Pisces Moon, you're also able to intuitively move through the world given your strong sixth sense. You're a doer and a dreamer, with an approach to life that blends together the practical and the emotional.
GEMINI	**PISCES**	With your Gemini Sun, learning is important to you. And with your Pisces Moon, the realms in which you're interested include understanding what moves, touches, and inspires people. Within you lives the eternal student and forever dreamer, which when aligned can be a beacon for healing and art that inspire others.
CANCER	**PISCES**	You have a natural aptitude to tune into the feelings circulating both around and within you. Maintaining boundaries, notably with your family, seems key to your happiness. As a Cancer Sun, your home is important, and your artistic Pisces Moon can help you make it a magically nurturing space.
LEO	**PISCES**	With your self-expressive Leo Sun and your muse-connecting Pisces Moon, you can be quite creative, apt to dive into the sea of artistry at a moment's notice. You're quite a romantic, someone who longs for love and experiences that deeply touch your heart.

☀ + ☾		PROFILE
VIRGO	**PISCES**	You strive to be of service, to help better the lives of others. With your Virgo Sun, you can craft solutions that address the concerns to which your compassionate Pisces Moon is attuned. Among your wide-spectrum skill set is your ability to see both the differences and similarities alive at once in any system.
LIBRA	**PISCES**	When it comes to relationships, you're a magic maker. Others are really attracted to you, as they sense you truly care about them. Both your harmony-revering Libra Sun and your pacific Pisces Moon cherish peace; while this helps you create beauty, it may also make you conflict avoidant at times.
SCORPIO	**PISCES**	Your approach to life embraces the belief that there is more to it than meets the eye. With your deep-diving Scorpio Sun and your soulful Pisces Moon, you love swimming in the sea of the numinous. Understanding your own motivations and helping others to do the same is a stellar healing power you have.
SAGITTARIUS	**PISCES**	You're a visionary on a mission, a philosopher who loves making sense of non-mundane matters. Your eyes are wide open and take in a spectrum of insights. With your exploratory Sagittarius Sun and your mystical Pisces Moon, you want to be unbound by constraints so that you can feel a greater sense of flow.
CAPRICORN	**PISCES**	While some people just envision fields of dreams, you've got the know-how to build them. You've got that winning combination of being able to marry pragmatism with imagination. When your hardworking Capricorn Sun has you bordering on burnout, trust your Pisces Moon to know how to invite relaxation into your life.
AQUARIUS	**PISCES**	Sometimes you may feel you're swimming in a different sea than many others. Between your future-forward Aquarius Sun and your know-no-bounds Pisces Moon, you can perceive things that others don't. You're an empathetic altruistic who dreams up ways to make the world a better place.
PISCES	**PISCES**	As a double Pisces, you love liminality, that space of the betwixt and between where both nothing and everything seem to exist. You are enchanted by things that appear filled with hope. Just watch that you don't get pulled under by waves of disillusionment when life doesn't match up to your romantic visions.

CHAPTER 24

THE MOON IN THE HOUSES

Our Moon sign gives us a stellar periscope into our emotional nature, what we need, and the instinctive ways in which we can take care of ourselves. We can gain further insights into how we can feel more at home in our life and in the world by looking at another factor in our birth chart: the house in which our Moon resides.

What's a "house"? When you look at an astrology chart—cast for the day, time, and place you were born—you will notice that it is divided into twelve pie pieces: these are the astrological houses. Originally called "places" (*topoi*) in ancient astrology, the houses represent the different areas that compose our life, including our relationships, careers, children, finances, health, creative pursuits, and all others.

When you look at your astrology chart, you will see that your Moon—and each of the other planets—is located in one of these twelve houses. While the sign signifies the style in which you express your Moon, it's the house that represents the arenas of your life in which you're most drawn to doing so. These are the realms in which you look for emotional fulfillment, where you feel nurtured, and where you seek comfort. Since the Moon relates to our instincts as well as the sense of feeling safe and secure, we often find ourselves with a natural affinity for the pursuits associated with the house in which our Moon is located.

Look below to find the house in which your Moon resides. There you will discover experiences that will have you feeling more nurtured, and which bring you greater ease, comfort, and joy. If you don't already know the house in which your Moon is located, see page 219 for a resource that will help you discover it.

Moon in the First House

- Feeling connected to your body
- Having a strong sense of personal style
- Being confident in how you carry yourself in life
- Having your emotions be recognized by others

Moon in the Second House

- Managing your finances
- Earning your own money
- Developing your skills and talents
- Valuing yourself and recognizing your self-worth

Moon in the Third House

- Being involved with your neighbors
- Communicating messages of import
- Learning languages and ways to express yourself
- Forging relationships with your siblings and/or cousins

Moon in the Fourth House

- Digging into your roots
- Feeling like you belong
- Being nurtured by your home
- Gathering with family, whether of origin or choice

Moon in the Fifth House

- Being creative
- Inviting in romance
- Connecting with children
- Having fun and amusement

Moon in the Sixth House

- Engaging with pets
- Focusing on your health
- Being satisfied by your work
- Mentoring others and/or being mentored

Moon in the Seventh House

- Forging alliances
- Being in relationships
- Working toward justice
- Negotiating agreements

Moon in the Eighth House

- Pooling resources
- Exploring intimacy
- Expressing yourself sexually
- Connecting to the mysteries of life

Moon in the Ninth House

- Setting goals
- Expanding your knowledge base
- Traveling and having adventures
- Delving into philosophy and spirituality

Moon in the Tenth House

- Contributing to society
- Maintaining your reputation
- Achieving your career goals
- Being recognized for your work

Moon in the Eleventh House

- Being part of a collective
- Using technology creatively
- Working toward a better future
- Connecting to your hopes and wishes

Moon in the Twelfth House

- Being soulful
- Going on retreats
- Exploring ancestral inheritances
- Spending time alone being quiet

CHAPTER 25

MOON MOMENTS

Not only does the Moon remind us of the cycles of life, it can also help us understand the different phases that we move through in ours. In addition to its sign and house placement, you can look to the Moon as a beacon to guide you through different moments of life's unfolding journey. The Moon can help us to better access awareness not only of our ever-changing needs, but also where we are in our own personal cycle of self-development. It can also help us to best align with the times, so that we feel like we're flowing with the currents of the current moment. There are numerous ways to look to the Moon for this wisdom. In this chapter, I will share three: the Lunar Return, Planetary Connections to the Moon, and Daily Moon Signs. To discover when these Moon Moments occur, see page 219 in the Resources section.

Lunar Return

"It's that time of the month" is a familiar refrain. When we say or hear it, we know that what's being referenced is the menstrual cycle, often a time of heightened sensitivity, both physically and emotionally. "It's that time of the month" also holds great power when we think about the Moon, notably in reference to the Lunar Return.

Every four weeks, the Moon undertakes a journey through all twelve zodiac signs. Once during its monthly sky-bound sojourn, it will cross the spot where it was when you were born. As it dwells there, you experience your Lunar Return. It's a moment when the collective emotional tenor seems to align with yours, sparking a resonance between your vibe and the cosmic vibe. During this monthly lunar homecoming, you may find yourself accessing an understanding of what it means to feel at home—in your body, family, and community, as well as in the way you contribute to the world around you. This awareness gifts you with more emotional clarity and resilience, treasures that can help you marshal the potential that your life offers.

As you discover the dates of your upcoming Lunar Returns, mark them on your calendar, perhaps with a symbol for the Moon. Then as each day arrives, consider carving out some space for the following:

SCHEDULE A NURTURING ACTIVITY

Allocate time for activities that you find nourishing, whether it's a walk in nature, a meal shared with friends, a visit to an art gallery, or any of the other pursuits that you find satisfying. (Explore ideas for activities that may be personally nurturing in the chapter dedicated to your Moon sign.) The Lunar Return is a wonderful day to cultivate a feel-good sense. Spending time doing activities you know will nurture you aligns with the opportunities that this day offers.

MAKE SPACE TO WITNESS YOUR EMOTIONS

Tune in to how you're feeling and what's striking a deep chord for you. Whether the day is filled with relaxation or a bevy of to-do list items, take a pulse on your moods and emotions. What's making you happy? Sad? Angry? Joyous? Acknowledge not only what you're feeling but also what's causing you to feel that way.

NOTICE AFFINITIES

Observe where you naturally flow, to whom and what you feel instinctively magnetized. Doing so will give you insights into the people, places, and things that offer you an innate sense of comfort. This will help you further perceive what experiences have you feeling supported, at home, and cared for.

CONTEMPLATE AND JOURNAL

Allocate some time to writing and/or drawing in your journal, capturing your sentiments on how you're feeling. Here are some Stellar Reflection Questions that you can use as journaling prompts:

- How am I feeling today?
- With whom do I want to spend time?
- What activities are drawing my attention?
- How would I describe what it feels like to feel at home?
- How is my sense of security being fostered or challenged?

When you find your Lunar Return dates, you will see that this monthly event actually occurs at a particular time. You don't have to do these activities at that precise moment; rather, you can do them several hours before or after. You can also give yourself a wider window, focusing on what's arising for you on a lunar level anytime during the 2.5 days that the Moon is in the same sign as yours.

Additionally, when you look for the dates of this monthly event, most astrology software programs and online calculators will cast a chart for your Lunar Return. Some astrologers work with these charts, finding them to provide insights into key themes that may unfold over the coming four weeks. If you're interested, you can find books and online resources that can teach you how to approach these charts, or you could consult with an astrologer who can give you monthly Lunar Return guidance.

Planetary Connections to the Moon

In addition to your Lunar Return, at additional moments other planets will connect to your Moon, dwelling at the same zodiacal spot that it resided when you were born. (In astrological parlance, this is called a "conjunction" and we say that a planet "conjoins" your Moon.) When this occurs, it marks a time when you're invited to make significant breakthroughs in your lunar consciousness, gaining awareness as to what nurtures and nourishes you.

Once you find the dates of these planetary connections, mark them on your calendar. Note that while the conjunction occurs at an exact moment, there's a window of time before and after in which you may experience it. That information is provided below, as is the frequency with which these events occur and the highlights of what they may call forth. (Throughout your life, in addition to the conjunctions, the planets will make other connections to your Moon. While these connections are not covered here, know that even though they do share some similarities with the conjunction, they also have their own unique qualities.)

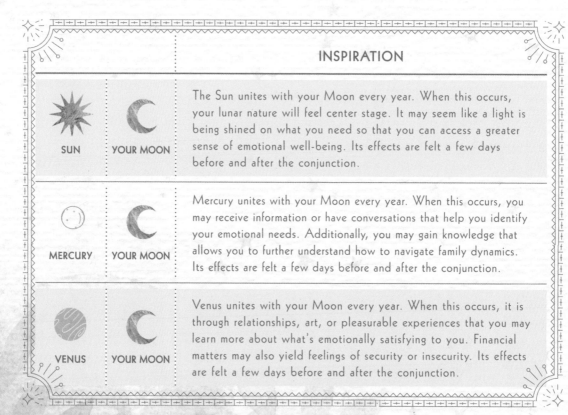

INSPIRATION

SUN / YOUR MOON	The Sun unites with your Moon every year. When this occurs, your lunar nature will feel center stage. It may seem like a light is being shined on what you need so that you can access a greater sense of emotional well-being. Its effects are felt a few days before and after the conjunction.
MERCURY / YOUR MOON	Mercury unites with your Moon every year. When this occurs, you may receive information or have conversations that help you identify your emotional needs. Additionally, you may gain knowledge that allows you to further understand how to navigate family dynamics. Its effects are felt a few days before and after the conjunction.
VENUS / YOUR MOON	Venus unites with your Moon every year. When this occurs, it is through relationships, art, or pleasurable experiences that you may learn more about what's emotionally satisfying to you. Financial matters may also yield feelings of security or insecurity. Its effects are felt a few days before and after the conjunction.

MARS	**YOUR MOON**	Mars unites with your Moon every two-plus years. When this occurs, while being in movement feels nurturing, it's important to not give in to bouts of impatience. Desires may be animating, and you can discover strategies that are most aligned with your needs. Its effects are felt several days before and after the conjunction.
JUPITER	**YOUR MOON**	Jupiter unites with your Moon every eleven to twelve years. When this occurs, it offers a concentrated experience to learn more about what you find nurturing and nourishing. There's a sense that you have more space to get your needs met. Since Jupiter relates to growth, just watch for a potential to gain weight. Its effects are felt a couple of weeks before and after the conjunction.
SATURN	**YOUR MOON**	Saturn unites with your Moon every twenty-nine to thirty years (with "reminders" every seven years). When this occurs, pruning away excess may feel necessary in order to better take care of yourself. It's a time in which emotional self-reliance and taking health issues seriously are emphasized. Its effects are felt at least a month before and after the conjunction.
URANUS	**YOUR MOON**	Uranus unites with your Moon every eighty-four years (with "reminders" every twenty-plus years). When this occurs, you may suddenly find yourself craving new experiences and having novel perspectives on your emotional needs and how to meet them. Unexpected events or realizations may encourage you to make big shifts in the landscape of your life as you redefine what it means to feel at home. Its effects are felt at least several months before and after the conjunction.

215

Note that sometimes the planets make several conjunctions to your Moon within a period of time. If that occurs, consider the activated period to begin before the first conjunction and to end after the final one. Additionally, you may also experience the conjunction of the other planets—Neptune and Pluto—to your Moon. Given that the length of their orbits (165 and 248 years, respectively) extends beyond an individual's life, though, many people never experience these astrological events. That said, even if they don't travel through the same zodiacal spot as your Moon, they're likely to make some connection to it over your life. As such, here's a quick note of what they may invite in when they align with your Moon: Neptune enhances sensitivity as well as the dissolving of boundaries, and Pluto invites us to go deeper and explore what's below the surface.

Daily Moon Signs

One way to tap into the zeitgeist of the moment is to look at the sign in which the Moon resides each day. Through its zodiacal placement, you can take the temperature on the collective vibe, gaining clarity on the currents of emotional tides that have a pull on all of us. By knowing the sign that the Moon is in, you can better assess the opportunities and challenges available, sequencing your activities and expectations throughout the month. The Moon moves through all twelve signs in about four weeks, spending about 2.5 days in each sign. Below you will find some aligned activities for each Moon sign day as well as things to look out for.

When the Moon's in Aries

■ Tap into your desires, marshal your will, and undertake a pioneering activity. Look out for impatience and bursts of anger.

When the Moon's in Taurus

■ Connect with nature, honor your senses, and focus on practical matters. Look out for stubbornness and a resistance to change.

When the Moon's in Gemini

■ Engage in conversations, learn new things, and share a message. Look out for information overload and capriciousness.

When the Moon's in Cancer

■ Connect with family, prepare food, and make your home cozier. Look out for the appearance of excess moodiness and defensiveness.

When the Moon's in Leo

■ Do creative projects, invite in more romance, and connect to your inner child. Look out for excessive pride and a heightened need for recognition.

When the Moon's in Virgo

■ Get organized, do crafts projects, and survey the details. Look out for heightened critical tendencies and a penchant for perfection.

When the Moon's in Libra

■ Get together with friends, beautify your environment, and negotiate agreements. Look out for indecision and excess indulgence.

When the Moon's in Scorpio

■ Explore intimacy, tune in to your deep feelings, and solve mysteries about things that intrigue you. Look out for power struggles and the desire to hide.

When the Moon's in Sagittarius

■ See the bigger picture, go on a quest, and connect to world cultures. Look out for zealousness and the desire to push beyond your limits.

When the Moon's in Capricorn

■ Envision career goals, review your finances, and attend to responsibilities. Look out for excess solemnity and burning the candle at both ends.

When the Moon's in Aquarius

■ Do a group activity, work on logistical solutions, and consider humanitarian issues. Look out for detachment and being too cerebral.

When the Moon's in Pisces

■ Let your imagination soar, perform random acts of kindness, and be inspired by art. Look out for blurred boundaries and giving away too much.

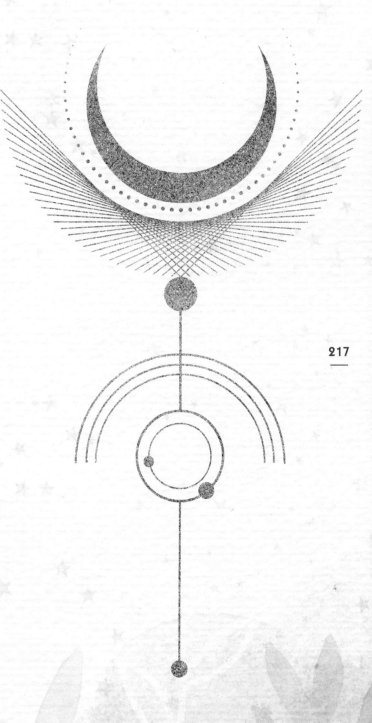

REFLECTIONS ON THE MOON

One of the many concepts that the Moon connects us to is the experience of coming full circle. After all, we end each month at a similar place that we began. The Moon is new and we, like Luna, are filled with promise and potential.

Reflecting that, while you are at the conclusion of *The Complete Guide to Living by the Moon*, I want to revisit what I shared at the beginning. I invite you to again think of the Moon and its ever-present yet ever-changing nature, and its role as a beacon, guide, and timekeeper.

Doing so, consider how your relationship with Luna has evolved from where it was when you set about to read this book compared to where it is now. Think not only about what you've learned about the Moon but also about yourself and others.

For example, in exploring the ways to align with the lunar cycle and manifest your intentions using Moon Mapping, what have you discovered about your own rhythms, what truly inspires you, and how to bolster your optimal well-being? And in learning about the astrological Moon, what new understanding do you now have related to your personal needs, how you orient emotionally, and the ways that you can best take care of yourself?

While you have reached the end of this book, hopefully it's just the beginning of your alliance with lunar-inspired living. As you navigate the shifting tides of life, its inherent joys as well as its challenges, may you take comfort in, gain strength from, and gather wisdom through your ongoing relationship with the Moon.

resources

To access dates for the lunar cycle, your lunar return, and Moon Moments, visit stephaniegailing.com/moon-resources. There you will also find ways to cast your chart and discover your Moon sign and the house in which it resides.

There are numerous books available through which you can learn about the Moon and the topics shared. Here are a few of my favorites:

Adler, Margot. *Drawing Down the Moon*. Penguin Books, 2006

Archive for Research in Archetypal Symbolism. *The Book of Symbols*. Taschen, 2010

Boland, Yasmin. *Moonology*. Hay House UK, 2016

Chevalier, Jean, and Gheerbrant, Alain. Translated from the French by John Buchanan-Brown. *The Penguin Dictionary of Symbols*. Penguin Books, 1997

Costello, Darby. *The Astrological Moon*. Raven Dreams Productions, 2017

George, Demetra. *Finding Our Way Through the Dark*. American Federation of Astrologers, 2008

George, Demetra. *Mysteries of the Dark Moon*. HarperOne, 1992

Greene, Liz and Sasportas, Howard. *The Luminaries*. Red Wheel / Weiser, 1992

Hand, Robert. *Planets in Transit*. Schiffer, 2002

Herring, Amy. *Astrology of the Moon*. Llewellyn, 2010

Holborn, Mark. *Sun and Moon*. Phaidon, 2019

Kane, Aurora. *Moon Magic*. Wellfleet, 2020

Lafranque, Stephanie. *Moon Energy*. Skyhorse, 2020

Marks, Tracy. *The Astrology of Self-Discovery*. Ibis Press, 2008

Paungger, Johanna and Poppe, Thomas. *The Power of Timing*. Wisdom Keeper Books, 2013

Rudyar, Dane. *The Lunation Cycle*. Aurora Press, 1967

Spiller, Jan. *New Moon Astrology*. Bantam Books, 2001

acknowledgments

The Complete Guide to Living by the Moon would not have come to life were it not for so many people who have shared their wisdom and encouragement with me throughout this creative journey:

Elizabeth You for her vision, understanding, and incredible editing skills. The amazing team at Wellfleet—including Publisher Rage Kindelsperger, Creative Director Laura Drew, Managing Editor Cara Donaldson, Art Director Marisa Kwek, and Marketing Manager Lydia Anderson—for creating this book and sharing it with the world. Artist Sosha Davis and designer Howie Severson for making it so beautiful. My husband Sebastiano for his unending love and support. My mother Bernice, and my grandmothers Sylvia and Hattie, for all the ways that they have guided and inspired me. Aimee Hartstein for our shared love of astrology. Heidi Lender, for our forever friendship. Megan Skinner for her wise counsel and invaluable contributions to the tarot card sections. Kim O'Donnel for her spirit and writing prowess. Tali Edut, Tony Howard, and Kate Petty who I not only adore but who have helped me give voice to my work over the years. Chavi Holm and Kim Colaprete for their kinship and generously offering Lake Diva for my writing retreat. Emily Blefeld, Dan Cohen, and the Seeing With Your Heart circle for the multivalent ways you support my creative expression. Simone, Ben, and Margot: I love you to the Moon and back. And finally, to the artists, explorers, astrologers, mystics, and healers whose connection with La Luna has informed mine.

about the author

Stephanie Gailing is a life guide, wellness astrologer, and author with more than 25 years of experience. Her unique approach to healing weaves together compassion-based coaching, self-care strategies, and astrological insights. In addition to working directly with individuals, couples, and organizations throughout the world, Stephanie regularly teaches workshops and writes about holistic well-being, inspiring her audience with ways to live their life with stellar awareness. Co-host of the *So Divine!* podcast, Stephanie is the author of *The Complete Book of Dreams*, *The Complete Guide to Astrological Self-Care*, and *The Astrological Self-Care Journal*. She holds a Certificate in EcoPsychology from Pacifica University, an Advanced Diploma in Coaching from New York University, and an MS in Nutrition from Bastyr University. You can find more about her work at StephanieGailing.com.

index